EVOLVING INTO MANHOOD

How to Think, Act and Grow into a Successful Man

By: Richard Celestin, Esq.

Copyright Page

To my Lord and Savior, Jesus Christ.

To my mother and father who sacrificed so much to
help me evolve into the man I am today.

To my sons, the J's, for being my greatest accomplishments.
I am excited to see the men you evolve into.

To all the men in my life who played a role in helping me
to navigate this journey called manhood.

Shoutout to my haters, doubters and for those waiting for me to fail.
Sorry but keep waiting!

For my sister, Cathiana. I love and miss you.

TABLE OF CONTENTS

FOREWORD

I have known Richard Celestin for more than a decade, meeting back in 2008 through a mutual friend. At the time I was a Youth Development Manager and supported multiple city public schools. This mutual friend mentioned Richard had this amazing debate program, the Young Debaters Program, geared towards students in grades six through twelve. The schools that I was supporting at the time did not have any debate programs. I was not only interested in introducing his program to the schools I supported but I was also inspired by his passion and vision. The goal of the program was to provide children with a platform to teach them lifelong skills and tools to express themselves through debate and advocacy. After having great success with middle and high school aged students, he offered the program to upper elementary school aged students. This allowed him to reach students at a very formative age and he was able to observe their growth as they progressed through middle and high school.

One of the chapters in this book (which happens to be my favorite) is titled "Ask for Help". In order for most young men to ask for help there must be a certain level of trust. In some cases, asking parents or caregivers for help can be difficult and/or embarrassing- it is incredibly challenging to be vulnerable! However, I believe asking for help shows strength. Opening the line of communication can be extremely beneficial - it not only helps with bonding but it also allows for effective communication, which ultimately can assist with steering or redirecting people down the right path. The chapter points out how a popular excuse for not asking for help is a feeling that "I can handle it on my own and don't need help". The fact of the matter is we all need help at some point in our lives. Young men sometimes have difficulty asking older men for advice. I am sure this book will dismiss that belief and serve as a source of motivation for young people to seek and obtain the support they need as they become men.

I have had the pleasure of serving as a judge at several debate competitions coordinated by Richard. The culminating event is exciting for the students, parents, educators, and judges. One competition in particular stands out. I remember a particular young man in middle school that presented a powerful argument with supporting facts and evidence who ultimately won the competition. His mother cried and told Richard and I that her son had a learning disability and that the competition was the first time that he was passionate about anything pertaining to education. In fact, she shared how the debate program kept him on track by teaching him how to structure, research and invest time in preparing his argument against his opponent. The school was reluctant to put him in the program but Richard wanted him to be part of the debate team because of the enthusiasm and desire he showed.

This is what Richard has and continues to do-shape young lives! Richard is a distinguished attorney and college professor, however, his passion and desire to support, nurture and change the lives of young adults is critical to him. His experiences working in the legal system daily has fostered his passion to help young men strive for better and to be greater. He lives for making change within young adults and college level students. For Richard, it is always about the 'why'. This work, this book, his day to day is his why!

In this book, Richard mentions his upbringing and things he has learned in his many years of experience working with young adults. The title of this book is "EVOLVING INTO MANHOOD: HOW TO THINK, ACT AND GROW INTO A SUCCESSFUL MAN". Although I have had positive role models in my life growing up, I could have benefited from this book. There were still questions I had about life and only felt comfortable asking close friends my age, who knew just a little as I did. I see this book as a resource guide that will bring value and structure to young men.

The title references the word success. Per Merriam Webster's dictionary, the definition of success is the accomplishment of an aim or purpose. This book provides an understanding of what an aim is and why it's important to have a purpose. If young men take heed to the tools Richard has provided, I am confident this will help develop or further develop the discipline it takes to follow the right path thus creating a better chance of "being successful".

-   Tariq McKay

CHAPTER 1

WHAT IS MANHOOD?

"Try not to become a man of success, but rather try to become a man of value."

-Albert Einstein

The word "manhood" has two core meanings- it is the adult period in a male human's life when he physically develops his male qualities, and then there's mental maturity. This dual meaning creates differing opinions regarding when a boy *actually* becomes a man.

For some, it is when the boy hits puberty. For others, it is when the boy begins to demonstrate responsibility and maturity in his actions and thought processes. For the purpose of this book, the focus will be on the latter. Manhood begins with the emotional, psychological and mental growth and evolution of a man, as opposed to the physical one.

Growing up in the 90's, and even today, boys of all ages were presented with a concept of manhood that was based on physical maturity and intense masculinity.

For instance, I grew up watching Arnold Schwarzenegger- the epitome of manhood at that time- defeat all enemies, human and alien. He showcased a rare physique that seemed like muscle on muscle.

I watched movies where men, with little to no emotion or cracks in their masculinity, put their bodies and their lives on the line to protect their families and loved ones. I grew up in a house with an amazing father who worked relentlessly to provide for his family but only saw him cry once- and even that didn't happen until I was well into adulthood.

Today, the concept of manhood continues to be presented in ways that do not align with mental, emotional and psychological growth.

Young boys are inundated with images of grown men expressing manhood through physical violence. Manhood is being presented as a concept more aligned with fear and intimidation rather than *respect* and *maturity*. In addition, the belief that "real men don't show emotion" adds to the misguided belief that men have to be strong and unemotional at all times, regardless of the circumstances.

Lastly, material wealth and idolization of items have somehow been connected with the concept of manhood. Through messaging in media, it is implied that the more money you have or material possessions you own, the more manly you are.

While these concepts of manhood have become so deeply rooted in society and the images we are presented, there is a recently growing shift in the view of manhood and what it encompasses.

Young boys are now being taught about the importance of developing the key ingredients of manhood. These key components go beyond external factors such as wealth, image or physique. After all, manhood still represents mental toughness and resilience while also demonstrating vulnerability, compassion and empathy.

As we begin to move away from society's representation of manhood and focus on the internal make-up of what a man really is, we will see a tremendous positive shift in our communities as it relates to the growth and development of young boys into men.

TOXIC MASCULINITY

In discussing the role that society plays in the (mis)understanding of manhood, it is essential to explore the concept of "toxic masculinity".

Toxic masculinity involves cultural and societal pressures for men to behave in a certain way in order to be a "real man". As mentioned previously, this includes the misconception that men have to be aggressive and tough while hiding emotion and vulnerability. This idea that men need to act tough and avoid showing all emotions can be harmful to the mental health of young boys and grown men. This will have extremely harmful effects on society, which is how it became known as "toxic masculinity."

Many researchers have identified the following 3 core components to toxic masculinity:

TOUGHNESS

The belief that men need to be physically strong and intimidating as well as aggressive. This is seen all too frequently when young boys are ready, willing and able to get into physical altercations due to someone looking at them wrong, bumping into them or scuffing their sneakers. The belief is that letting one of these incidents slide is a sign of weakness which is a direct attack on their perceived definition of manhood

ANTIFEMININITY

The belief that men need to reject anything that is seen as being feminine. This includes showing emotion or demonstrating vulnerability. The more common way I have seen this in my work with young people, and with adult men, is how quickly an action, comment or thought is classified as being feminine or not manly if it is presented in any way that shows weakness or is attached to anything deemed to be unmanly.

POWER

The belief that masculinity and manhood are directly connected to power and status, which includes financial and social status. The need to amass material possessions and achieve popularity, particularly among women, is a classic example of the misguided interpretation of what manhood is. Often times the need to work so hard to externally show power is often connected to a need to mask or hide internal insecurities.

As these concepts have been normalized amongst young men, they continue to grow and manifest into the harmful views and behaviors we may see in adult men.

One major area of concern is the male view of mental health. Toxic masculinity generally discourages men from getting mental health treatment. Depression, anxiety and related mental health problems are generally viewed as weakness. Talking about and seeking help for these thoughts of insecurity are frowned upon and often result in holding in and holding back feelings which can create deeper states of depression and loneliness.

CONTROL YOUR EVOLUTION

As a boy evolves and develops into a man it is essential to understand not only how important this development is but also how personal it is as well. You are in control of your evolution. This means that the characteristics and make-up of who you are as a man is fully within your control. You must navigate your journey and become the person you wish to be and whom the people closest to you wish for you to become. In doing so you must not worry about confirming to what society says you must do or allow peer pressure to influence your decisions and growth. Your evolution into manhood is a personal journey and one you must be focused on by maintaining that your best interest is above all else.

I was very intentional in using the word "evolve" in the title of this book. I was considering using the word "grow" but decided against it. The reason is that I do not want to confuse the idea that being big and tall makes you a man. I have met some middle school students who are taller than most adults I know. Being a man is not about your height or weight. It is about the ingredients you possess internally and how you exude them externally.

As you grow older, the main ingredients of manhood will grow and change. Your actions become more intentional and purposeful. This transition is best described using the word evolution. To evolve means to develop gradually, especially from a simple to a more complex form. This is the path to manhood. This is the path to success.

•••

The purpose of this book is not to dictate what your evolution should look like. Instead, the goal is to guide you along in your personal journey.

I understand that the evolution can be a challenge if there is not adequate support and guidance through the process.

This book is designed to present some empowering and powerful characteristics that should remain the focus as we learn and embrace the journey of manhood.

Some of these characteristics are more required than optional and you will understand that as you make your way through the book. As you seek to evolve into the manhood, this book will support you in creating the best version of yourself possible.

That best version of you is the man this world needs!

CHAPTER 2

FOUNDATION OF MANHOOD

"A man is one whose body has been trained to be the ready servant of his mind; whose passions are trained to be the servants of his will; who enjoys the beautiful, loves truth, hates wrong, loves to do good, and respects others as himself."

–John Ruskin

The most important aspect of building a house is first laying a solid and strong foundation. With a strong foundation, an amazing house can be built that can survive for many years.

This book will share and explain the characteristics of manhood while this chapter will lay the foundation of it.

By "foundation" in this context, I am referring to the set of principles that will direct your focus as you navigate the journey into manhood. Understanding where your focus and intent lie will ensure growth and success as a man.

Intent remains one of my favorite concepts from law school. Intent is simply the state of mind with which an act is done, specifically

17

focusing on if the act is done with and on purpose.

In life, we must move and operate with intention and purpose. Our thoughts, our actions and our plans for the future must all be directed by our intention. Intention is very subjective and based on the goals of the individual. For example, an individual aiming to lose weight makes intentional decisions throughout the course of the day that guided by that desire. *Do I take the elevator or stairs? Eat a salad or fast food? Exercise or watch television?*

Similarly, as boys it is essential to move and act with intention as you evolve into men. You must know your purpose.

While the goal is to move with intent and purpose, this can be difficult for the average young boy.

The reason lies in human development, specifically within the brain. The pre-frontal cortex, the part of the brain responsible for impulse control, consequential thinking and forward planning; is not fully developed until an individual is around twenty-four years old. Not only does this make it challenging for young men to create a plan focused on moving with intention but it also makes it challenging for them to listen to the advice of adults who stress this point as well.

My hope is that this book, as presented in the most straight-forward and basic way, can attempt to break this mentality and create trust in the advice and insight presented by elders, mentors, parents, and role models.

DEFINE YOURSELF ON YOUR TERMS

Defining yourself- *who you are, what you stand for, what you believe-* is essential in developing the character, personality and morals needed to be a successful man.

Unfortunately, more now than likely at any other point, it is incredibly difficult to do so for young people. In addition to adults telling young people who to be and how to act, there is the tremendous role of social media that greatly influences young people and how they choose to define themselves.

Being your true self, independent of the opinions of others and with little to no interest in conforming to other people's definition of you, is the key to defining yourself on your own terms. Living a life driven by whether people like you or not or how many likes or followers you have in a fake digital world will only lead to feeling empty and living a lie. The world does not need any more copies or imitations- the world needs a real and authentic you!

IN WORD AND DEED

Imagine if I told you I wanted to join a sports team and become the best player on the team. Most people would be happy and excited for my plan.

Now imagine that while telling you this, I showed more interest in playing video games than practicing, started to eat French fries and hamburgers daily instead of healthier foods, or watched cartoons all day instead of studying films about the sport. I imagine at some point you would question my plan based on my actions.

In life it is very easy to talk a great game about what you want to do, plan to do, or intend to do. The hard part is aligning your actions with your words. At the end of the day, actions speak louder than words. Knowing that, spend less time announcing to people what your plan is or what you intend on doing and focus on actually *doing* it.

One of my favorite lines from the artist Lil Wayne that I use all the time is "real G's move in silence like lasagna". Let your actions speak for itself but if you announce a plan or intention, follow through with it until completed.

SCHOOL IS PRETTY COOL

A particular issue I see among young men is that being smart or involved in one's education is looked down upon. School is often seen as uncool and being too involved may lead to name calling or bullying. I see this particularly when academic opportunities present themselves for students and it is primarily young ladies that take advantage of them.

This is not a new concept as I remember being a young man and witnessing the same issue (as I often sat out of academic activities too).

The reality is that being intelligent, taking advantage of educational opportunities, and excelling in school go well beyond being cool or uncool.

Being the cool kid in elementary, middle or high school means absolutely nothing in the grand scale of life. It is not an indicator of the level of success you will ever achieve in life. The momentary gratification we get for being popular in school has very little impact on how well we will evolve into our destined manhood.

However, your education and how you approach your studies along with the plan you create to map out your future and career matter without question. If you have a plan for the future and it requires gaining superior skills, experience, and knowledge- gear up to learn every bit of it that you can.

Education is important to thriving in any respective area you wish to maintain a career in. Success requires excelling in school at your earliest of stages. Do not be afraid to do what you have to do to move in the direction of excellence.

You do not need validation or approval from anyone to be the best student you can be. This journey is yours!

ANALYZE YOUR CIRCLE OF FRIENDS

Your circle of friends are the people that you are likely to spend the most time with. They will play a role in your day-to-day decisions as well as your plans for the future, short and long term.

Recognizing the impact that our circle of friends has on our intention and purpose is important to our evolution. You want to make sure you have a supportive and empowering circle.

If your circle includes people who discourage you from growing, encourages your engagement in harmful behavior, and does not support you unconditionally then it is time to re-evaluate and make changes to your circle.

In addition, it may be time for you to redefine who and what you consider a friend. Your circle should want you to win. Your circle should clap the loudest when you accomplish a goal or have good news. Your circle should always want the best for you and push you to achieve your best in all things. If your circle does not do this, you need a new circle.

SET GOALS AND ATTACK THEM

Setting goals, both short-term and long- term, help us to define our intention and purpose and guide us in our daily decisions. Each day is an opportunity to move closer to our goals- what we elect to do with those opportunities is up to us.

Operating without goals is like walking around in circles and wondering how or why you have not accomplished anything or moved forward. The enemies of achieving goals are procrastination and setting unmanageable goals- such as goals too vague or that are unaligned with our interests or passions. As well, we are allowing outside forces to influence our path to achieving our goals. These are some obstacles that an individual may face while goalsetting- from young people to accomplished professionals.

The difference is that with maturity and experience, anyone is able to overcome these obstacles and hurdles.

One method to conquering goals is to write them down and include their deadline. This allows one to visualize themselves accomplishing the goals,

You must fall in love with the feeling of success, ask for help if and when necessary, spend less time focusing on the negative or what is going wrong, and invest more time in positive and empowering thoughts.

People who set and accomplish goals are not special. They just know how to approach goal setting and execution.

S.M.A.R.T GOALS

The basic equation to goal setting and execution is following the S.M.A.R.T. Method of goal setting. This involves mapping out your goals so that they are:

SPECIFIC
the more detailed your goal the easier it is to work towards it

MEASURABLE
in order to know if you are progressing towards your goal you need to know how to measure growth

ATTAINABLE
make sure the goal you set is possible to reach based on the parameters you set

RELEVANT
accomplishing the goal means significantly more to you than working towards something else

TIME SENSITIVE
you must set a deadline otherwise you will always be working and never complete your goal

QUESTION EVERYTHING

One of the most important skills any good lawyer needs is the ability to ask meaningful and thought-provoking questions. In asking these questions, we gather the information that we need to direct our next move. I encourage everyone to ask questions for the purposes of seeking the truth and getting to the core of any matter.

Unfortunately, the concept of questioning has been presented as, and deemed to be, disrespectful by many. Compounding this issue is the fact that we live in a "cut and paste" society- due to social media- and are in a unique situation where young people believe whatever is presented. Many audiences do not seek to find the truth or attempt to discover a deeper meaning. This has led to a world full of misconception and misinformation.

To be an effective critical and creative thinker, it is essential to ask questions. Little kids love to ask "why"- not out of disrespect but instead out of genuine curiosity and a need to learn new things.

This can and should be done at any time to understand why. There is no need to struggle to find answers. Simply ask- purposefully and respectfully- with a clear goal in mind.

For example, when I tell my son to clean and organize his room, I respect that he asks me "why?" I want him to understand the purpose of why it is important so I present my reasoning. If I am unable to explain why, or the only response available is, "I told you so," I have failed in educating him on the importance of seeking understanding. It is important for a child of any age to learn how to find purpose in questions and actions.

EMBRACE FEAR

"Fear kills more dreams than failure ever will." Think about that.

You cannot possibly succeed at anything if you do not even try from the beginning. Many people tend not to want to try or take risks due to the fear of failing and the negative feelings associated with failing. This includes being judged, not feeling good enough, etc.

When faced with fear, there are essentially two options- fight or flight. If you choose flight, or basically running away from the thing that fears you, you run the risk of normalizing that behavior. Plus, you never know if the thing you scared of is not something you may eventually grow to love. For example, have you ever tried a food that you avoided for so long only to find out that you love it?

If you chose fight, then you place yourself in a situation where you can really learn about who you are and what you are made of. By fighting, you choose to stand for what you believe in and what you are pursuing and not allow anyone or anything to get in the way. In life we will constantly be placed in a situation of fight or flight, especially if you have an ambitious set of goals or career plans.

Embrace that fear will be a part of every big decision and huge risk you will take. Understand that fear is not a sign you should run but instead it is notice that you need to be your strongest and bravest version to push forward and succeed.

BE SELFISH (FOCUS ON YOU)

Since kindergarten, we have all been taught the value and importance of sharing and not being selfish. I wholeheartedly believe in the power of giving and being selfless but in reality there is also a healthy amount of selfishness that is needed to succeed.

To be clear, when I encourage being selfish I do not mean looking to harm anyone or not being charitable. By selfish, I mean, be sure you focus more energy on your growth and development than anything else. In actuality, an investment in self has the ultimate goal of putting you in a position to better help others.

For anyone who has ever been on a plane, I imagine you are familiar with the pre-flight instructions provided by the steward or stewardess. In addition to the seatbelt instructions and the life jacket demonstration, there is an explanation of the use of the oxygen masks. It is explained that in the event of a change in cabin pressure oxygen masks will fall in front of you. You are then directed to "put your mask on first" before helping anyone sitting next to you.

At first this sounds incredibly selfish. You are being told to ignore the person next to you that you may love more than anyone else and instead focus on putting your mask on. While this may seem selfish, in reality you are required to be selfish in the moment in order to be selfless later. If you do not have your mask on and cannot breathe then you cannot possibly help the person you care about next to you. However, by putting your mask on and ensuring that you are able to breathe comfortably then you can turn and help others.

I imagine most people at their core have a desire to help others. You cannot help others if you are not in a position of personal health, safety and comfort. You cannot reach this position unless you put yourself, your health, your mental well-being and your growth first and foremost. As your foundation gets stronger you can build, grow and help anyone and everyone you care about.

CHAPTER 3
FAMILY FIRST ALWAYS

"Family isn't always blood. It's the people in your life who want you in theirs; the ones who accept you for who you are. The ones that would do anything to see you smile and who love you no matter what."

-Anonymous

One of the most popular movie franchises in recent times is the Fast and Furious franchise. The main character, Dom Torreto, played by Vin Diesel, is the leader and plays the role of the alpha male. While his affinity for cars and violence are typical characteristics of an alpha male character in a movie (and real life), there is one thing that is most important to him- family.

One of his most notorious lines in the franchise is "I don't have friends- I have family". Throughout the movie series, he goes above and beyond to protect his family at all costs. This concept of family is a running theme throughout the movie franchise and is at the foundation of what it means to be a man.

Let me start by being clear about what family means. The traditional definition of family

29

is: one or more parents and their child or children living together as a unit.

The reality is that while this definition holds true in some cases, it is not, by far, the all-encompassing definition of family. Today, *family* looks very different by definition and within a household. Households are now made up of legal guardians, grandparents, uncles, aunts and many more variations.

Beyond the household, the saying still holds true that blood does not necessarily make you family. Sometimes the people that are blood related to us are the ones we have the unhealthiest relationships with. Other times, people we are not related to may be the ones who show us unconditional love and support.

Family is both loosely defined but strictly enforced and protected. This is important to understand so any reader who does not have a "traditional" family unit understands that they still have family to love and protect.

FAMILY FIRST

The concept of "family first" can have many interpretations. When I work with young people, I use it in a very specific and strategic way.

I often find that young people, particularly boys, tend to engage in harmful behavior when in front of an "audience" encompassing negative peer support and behaviors.

This "audience" typically consists of friends who, whether through peer pressure or lack of maturity, engage in or encourage this behavior. The result is usually bad.

I often ask, "Who do you love more than anyone else?" And while responses vary, it is typically a loved one or family member. Finally I ask, *how do they feel their loved one would respond to such negative and harmful behavior?* Seeing the connection being made in the facial expression is priceless and means I have presented a very valuable lesson on consequential thinking.

WHAT FAMILY FIRST MEANS

"Family First" thinking as I present it, is focused on evaluating your actions in light of how your family would respond. *Would your family approve of your actions or be disappointed or hurt? Do your actions in any way benefit or hurt your family?*

These questions need to take priority over whether or not your friends will think you are cool, if they will find it funny, or even worse- if your actions will get likes or follows on social media.

Family first means considering your family when acting, planning and growing. Thinking of your loved one should always be factored into deciphering what is in your best interest. As well, this should be in the best interest of those who truly care about you.

Keep in mind that when you achieve great success, it will often be your family applauding the loudest. If you experience hardships or challenges, it will be your family that will often be there to pick you up and show love. Making your family proud must take priority over appeasing anyone else.

CONTRIBUTE IN THE HOUSE

Some young men are not in a position to contribute to the house financially due to their age, academic priorities, and inability to work.

However, financial contribution is just one of many ways in which help and support can be provided to your family. Depending on the make-up of your circumstances, it goes well beyond money and more about showing gratitude and being helpful.

One way is in completing chores. Yes, I said doing chores!

Wash the dishes, clean up your room, throw out the garbage, clean up after any pets- these are all invaluable ways to pay back your family for the love and support they provide to you. For those who have younger siblings, be a role model by helping to support your siblings as much as possible. Look out for your parents and do the small things necessary to make their lives easier.

It can be as simple as serving someone in your family a glass of water or taking the initiative to do a task without having to be told. Family is all about loving and supporting each other.

Contributing in meaningful ways not only shows love, but adds value to your role and existence as a young man and future head of household. Additionally, being a helpful family member while you are young builds the necessary foundation of servitude for the future- if and when you decide to have your own family.

UNPLUG AND CONNECT IN REAL LIFE

The appeal and lure of social media is something that is a real issue to both adults and kids alike. It is very easy to spend more time connected to an imaginary world than to build real-life connections, especially with family.

Too often I see families at dinner in restaurants and the kids are on their phones while the adults are either talking among themselves or just staring at the table. Young people in general need to understand and appreciate how precious time is and how important it is to invest that time in something meaningful and rewarding like family.

It is possible to disconnect from the virtual world for an hour or two and focus on your family. Even better, take the initiative to create the rules during family time for everyone, adults included, to disconnect and enjoy the precious moment amongst one another.

CHAPTER 4

GIVE AND GET RESPECT

*"I'm not concerned with you liking
or disliking me.
All I ask is that you respect me like a human being."*

– Jackie Robinson

Respect is a concept that is often heard but not easily described. It is easy to identify when respect is lacking but it is challenging to define what respect is or what it looks like. A very simple and basic definition of respect is accepting someone or something for who they are and what they are about. It is important to note that part of this definition of respect does not include that one has to like or agree with a person or their viewpoint but it is about accepting that person's position or opinion regardless.

Today, arguably more than at any other point in history, there is daily conflict that challenges our ability to accept and respect others. Our opinions and thoughts are often so strong and so biased that the concept of respecting someone who disagrees with that opinion seems impossible.

Unfortunately, this lack of respect is not limited to a mental position but can quickly lead to physical attacks or threats. The idea that someone is willing to harm someone else due to a disagreement in thoughts or opinions is truly the epitome of a lack of respect. However, as noted before, we can easily identify when respect is lacking.

My focus for this chapter is to discuss how to show respect. To truly understand, it is important to break it down its two core parts- self-respect and respect for others.

SELF-RESPECT

At the core of respecting others is knowing how to respect yourself. If you do not know how to respect yourself, or understand the importance of self-respect, then respecting others will be a challenge.

Dignity is the state or quality of being worthy of respect through a sense of pride in oneself. Developing dignity is at the core of appreciating respect and valuing the importance of giving it to others. At the core of dignity are certain key values that are necessary to developing self-respect:

> ### Be an Honest Person
>
> The best version of you is someone who has values and morals and follows through on them in both word and deed.

Always Strive to Reach Your Potential

Work your hardest and challenge yourself while keeping in mind that you are your only competition!

Accept Yourself and Your Gifts

The best part about you is that there is only one of you. Accept all aspects of who you are and your uniqueness in order to understand your gift to this world.

Be Kind to Yourself

Self-criticism and constantly seeking perfection is very harmful. Be very careful of how you use the words "I am" when describing yourself.

Be Humble

Act in ways because it is the right thing to do rather than seeking validation or praise from others. Be selfless.

Stand Up For Yourself

Know your value as a person and do not allow others to treat you as any less. Stand up for yourself by not being confrontational, but instead by being assertive. Know when you are not appreciated or respected & walk away.

> **Treat Others the Way You Expect to Be Treated**
>
> Leading by example is a great way to show and receive respect while also maintaining a level of maturity and dignity.

> **Focus On Internal Love and Validation**
>
> Love yourself and praise yourself independent of outside factors and influence, especially social media and friends.

As with most things in life, we must focus on the things that are within our control. By doing so, we will be prepared to address, respond to, and handle situations and circumstances that are beyond our control.

Working on and developing self-respect is at the core of understanding how to respect others and appreciate the respect that is given. It teaches us to recognize what respect is and how it feels rather than becoming experts on knowing when respect is lacking.

RESPECT OTHERS

Showing respect to others is a win-win situation for those who do it and do it right.

The reason why, is because not only does showing respect strengthen relationships and builds bonds but it also allows us to learn about ourselves and find ways to grow our own self-respect. When the people we interact with feel respected and understood, they return a similar level of reverence which results in positive relationship building and stronger connections.

Before I jump into the various ways in which we can show respect to others, I want to focus on what I believe is the main reason people tend to show disrespect- the false notion that respect is conditional.

My parents raised me to be respectful to everyone. This was shown in various ways from greeting people when I enter a room, shaking hands when appropriate, and holding the door open for the person coming after me.

One of my biggest pet peeves is when I hold the door open for someone and I do not receive an acknowledgement or "thank you". Despite my frustration in circumstances like this, I continue to hold the door open for people regardless. I can easily decide to stop being so kind and justify it by believing that many people may not care to recognize it or even return the favor if roles were reversed. However, I always default to the lessons I learned from my parents to show respect even if it is not shown to me. I do not need acknowledgement in order to do the right thing by showing respect.

Respect is unconditional and should be given regardless of the circumstances. When someone chooses not to acknowledge your respectful manner, do not let them deter you from being your best self.

Showing respect is a learned behavior that many have not been taught. When you show respect, it is a reflection of who you are and should not be misconstrued by the actions of others.

If someone elects to show lack of respect to you, your responsibility is to maintain your higher position of respect. Do not lower yourself to meet that person where they are.

A huge part of being mature is not allowing others to so easily move you from your position. To be clear- I understand how incredibly difficult this can be, particularly for young men who are constantly being evaluated on their manhood and toughness. When placed in these challenging situations, it is important to remember who *you* are.

Stand firm in the morals that are important to you, the people who are expecting you to act in a respectful manner, the things you risk losing, and the potential consequences by acting in a disrespectful way.

Demonstrating respect toward others may vary depending on differing situations. There is no universal method of showing respect and often will encompass multiple actions and approaches. Below are some key examples of how you can show respect to others in a meaningful and positive way.

Listen to Others, Don't Just Hear Them

Hearing is the process of recognizing sound, while listening is about giving what you hear thoughtful attention. Listening to others entails paying attention, processing what is being said and engaging them in meaningful conversation.

Show Empathy

We do not have to be directly impacted by a situation to show care or concern for those who are directly impacted. The mentality of "it doesn't affect me so it's not my problem" is one of the core issues with so much division and conflict in our communities and throughout the world.

Disagree Respectfully

Not everyone you interact with is going to share your same views, values or opinions. Honestly, that is a great thing because life would be very boring if everyone thought the exact same way. Rather than criticize or insult someone for having a position different than yours, acknowledge their position and try to learn from their perspective. Worst case scenario, you can agree to disagree and keep it moving.

Show Gratitude and Appreciation

If we have learned anything over the course of the last few years it is that life is incredibly precious and short. We must take every opportunity we can to acknowledge and show appreciation for those people in our lives that love and support us unconditionally. This includes parents, friends, teachers, community members- anyone and everyone who has and continues to help and support you. A "Thank you" means so much and is so easy to say.

Focus on the Small Things

Respecting others is not just about the big overt acts but it is also found in the small details that we often take for granted. Firmly shake someone's hand when you meet them. Look a person in the eye when speaking with them. Be polite and courteous. Ask people how they are doing and not only mean it but intend on hearing a response. Use people's names when addressing them. These are all small but truly effective ways to show respect to people on a daily basis that takes little to no effort.

At the core of a positive and empowering society is respect. It is essential for a happy and healthy relationship, necessary for a positive and meaningful friendship, and at the core of a productive school environment and workplace. Learning the value and importance of respect in every interaction and relationship is at the key to tremendous self-growth as well as taking part in making your school, your community, and the world a better place.

CHAPTER 5

HARD WORK IS NOT AN OPTION

"It's not about money or connections – it's the willingness to outwork and outlearn everyone."

– Mark Cuban

Regardless of how you choose to define success or the goals you ultimately set for yourself, at the center of achieving either is *hard work*.

Hard work is a necessity, not an option, on the path to success. At the foundation of every success story presented is *hard work* and a *commitment* to do the small things that other people are not willing to do to ensure success. This includes sacrifice, staying up later, waking up earlier, asking for help and never giving up!

Hard work looks different for different people and is not something that can or should be compared. You define your own hard work and success!

Hard work looks different based on individual goals and approaches. It is difficult to develop one universal definition so each person should work to define it personally. We often hear things like being resilient, staying dedicated, making sacrifices when necessary and much more related and powerful insight.

In my opinion, the most universal understanding of hard work is related to acknowledging your potential at all times. It is in knowing that you are putting 100% of yourself in a task or project that defines what hard work is.

It is in recognizing that your only competition is you and your goal is to find ways to outwork yourself each day. When you are blessed with an ability to work hard, opportunities to achieve success present themselves. The people around you get ready and willing to support you.

Failure to work to your greatest potential is like wasting your talent. A famous line from a great movie, *The Bronx Tale*, says it best- "the saddest thing in life is wasted talent".

I will put this in a practical and personal example. My oldest son is currently in high school and has consistently been an honor student. Let's say that one day he brings home a 70 on an exam and presents it to me. I am not going to react to the grade, but instead I will ask a few questions before reacting.

My focus is related to whether my son studied and how much effort he put into preparing for the exam. If my son says that he studied hard and practiced and despite the preparation he got that 70, then I will be satisfied- not with the grade but with his effort and ability to work towards his potential regardless of the results. If, however, my son says that he did not study, then we will have a problem.

In that case, the poor grade is a direct reflection of his lack of effort in working towards his potential and what he is capable of doing. Negligent effort is unacceptable in my book, and a mentality that I am working hard to rid from the minds of youth.

• • •

In my experience, there are four key obstacles to hard work. I want to explore these obstacles and discuss their importance. It is important to understand why energy needs to be invested to overcome these obstacles in order to achieve success on your terms.

1. AVOID COMPLACENCY

Often when we get upset or comfortable with our current situation, but refuse to work to improve, we are being complacent. A complacent person never works to reach their potential because they feel that it is pointless. The comfort level that we experience in staying in an unhealthy position may be too appealing. It is in fighting through complacency and getting out of our comfort zone that we not only grow, but also learn what we are truly made of and are capable of achieving. In everything we do, the goal is to continue to push ourselves to see how much further we can go.

My story of success starts from a place of complacency. A few years after graduating from law school, I was working a full-time job that was fun but easy. I was making decent money and was incredibly comfortable investing more time in hanging out and watching television than working on myself or figuring out my next challenge.

One day, after a very unchallenging day at work, I was sitting at home watching television eating a huge bowl of pasta. I asked myself whether or not I was fulfilled and realized that I was incredibly unhappy.

The source of my unhappiness was in knowing in my core that I was not working towards my potential and was in a deep state of complacency. Within two weeks of that day, I quit my job and applied for a new and more challenging position. This was the start of the process that led me to start my own business. From here on out, I began setting meaningful goals to work towards. I have never looked back since!

A misconception that I have often been presented with that deals with complacency is the belief that constantly seeking new goals and new heights translates to a lack of appreciation for the accomplishments achieved. This is absolutely not the case. It is completely possible to be thankful for and appreciative of achieving a goal while still desiring to reach for the next.

It is not about greed or arrogance but instead is a natural need or desire to keep growing, get stronger, and work to reach our greatest potential. You will never know what you are capable of until you push yourself to what you believe are your limits and keep going.

2. PRACTICE DELAYED GRATIFICATION
(AVOID SHORT CUTS)

Advancements in technology, specifically as it relates to the development and growth of smart phones, has had a tremendous beneficial impact on the world. However, it has also impacted our thought process and expectations in a significantly negative way.

We are now accustomed to things taking place in an instant- getting information, communicating with people, downloading content and so much more. The ability to get what we want almost instantaneously has crossed over into our expectations in life.

Many people now expect results, rewards, and successes quickly with little to no investment in time or energy. This need for instant gratification causes people to sacrifice plans and goals to try to find quick and easy ways to achieve success sooner rather than later. In doing so, the feeling of happiness related to the success achieved is short-lived. As Zig Ziglar once said- "be careful not to compromise what you want most for what you want now!"

Delayed gratification is defined as the act of resisting an impulse to take an immediately available reward in the hope of obtaining a more- valued reward in the future.

Exercising self-control and waiting for a delayed satisfaction is less attractive than an immediate satisfaction or result. Learning to manage impulses is a skill necessary in childhood but equally as important, and with greater potential risks and rewards, in adulthood. Choosing to study over going out to play with friends, saving money over buying something you may not need, and furthering your education to get a career over getting a job quicker are all examples of delayed gratification.

Mastering this skill can lead to the achievement of much greater rewards and goals.

3. BUILD RESILIENCE

There are few things in life that are a guarantee for anyone and everyone. One of those guarantees in life is that everyone, at some point or another, will face adversity, obstacles, challenges and failure. It is unavoidable no matter how hard you try.

Resilience is our ability to adapt and bounce back when we face hardships and challenges in life. Resilient people don't wallow or dwell on failures; they acknowledge the situation, learn from their mistakes, and move forward.

As often heard, it is not about how many times we get knocked down but how many times we get back up. The way to win is to keep fighting. Working hard is just that- hard. There are times when you will question why you are working so hard or struggle to overcome difficult challenges. You may even reach moments when quitting seems more appealing than doing the work. It is in these moments that our resilience is tested.

While there are many different approaches to developing resilience, I believe one of the most important and effective approaches involves managing and controlling your perspective. For resilient people, failure and obstacles are not barriers but instead opportunities- opportunities to grow, opportunities to get stronger and opportunities to learn how badly we want to succeed. Analyzing the causes and results of setbacks with positivity and optimism is essential for resilience.

Equally as important is recognizing what is within our control and what is not. We must focus our time and energy on the things we can control.

A famous and incredibly relevant quote to live by is, "life is 10% what happens to you and 90% how you react to it!"

4. DO NOT BE AFRAID TO FAIL

Fear of failure is often a barrier in working towards one's potential. Fear is known to stunt growth and limit one's ability to push beyond the limits. No one enjoys failing and the risk of it is significantly minimized when we stay within our comfort zone. In these cases, we may avoid taking risks or pushing hard enough to grow. However, while we minimize the risk of failing by staying safe, we also minimize our ability to grow and see what we are capable of doing.

Hall of Fame hockey player Wayne Gretzky said it best- "we miss 100% of the shots that we do not take".

Behind every great personal success story, there will be a fear of failure or falling short. This should not serve as a barrier to your efforts or goals. These feelings are normal. I have often been told that if my dreams and goals do not scare me a little, I am not dreaming or planning big enough.

Fear of failure is completely normal and comes with every goal or ambition we possess. However, the desire to achieve that goal should always outweigh the fear of not achieving it. Fear should never stop you from trying to push yourself to your limit and beyond. I was always told that if your goals or dreams do not scare you a little bit then you are not dreaming big enough.

CHAPTER 6

CONTROL THE VOLUME

"What lies behind us and what lies before us are tiny matters compared to what lies within us."

- Ralph Waldo Emerson

It is safe to assume that most people listen to music. I assume in most of those situations when we do listen to music we are in control of the songs we listen to and the volume in which we listen to them. When a song comes on that we love for whatever reason, (makes us feel good, moves our body, helps us remember the happy times, etc.) the natural reaction is to turn the volume up and consume as much of that good feeling as possible. However, when a song comes on that we dislike or makes us feel bad or sad we are faced with a different feeling and reaction.

While there are numerous options, including skipping or removing the song, a natural reaction is to also turn the volume down. We want to avoid taking in those negative feelings and thoughts in light of how they make us feel. These natural reactions are examples of how we protect ourselves, our thoughts and our feelings through something as simple as listening to music.

Applying this approach and mentality to life is more challenging but serves the same, and greater, purpose.

Controlling the volume on a more practical level in life goes beyond listening to music. It is about controlling the intake and influence of those things that affect how we think, feel and act in both positive and empowering ways as well as in negative and harmful ways. This is an essential skill for young people who are constantly being evaluated and judged by peers. Young people may be willing to do anything to conform to what people want or expect of them over their own self-interests.

Evolving into manhood is recognizing that the "noise" will not stop, and if anything will *increase* with success. The goal is managing the "noise" and, in many cases, drowning it out with positivity and love. The true power lies in understanding that you are in control of what you intake and how it affects you.

I learned the value of this skill on a smaller level when I was a kid. While I was rarely afraid of horror movies, there was one particular movie which scared me tremendously- Jaws. It was about a deadly shark that seems to prey on a family.

I remember as a kid having nightmares that resulted in me waking my parents up at all hours of the night. One night my mother taught me a skill that not only stopped the nightmares but also planted the seed to understanding the value of controlling the volume.

She asked me where my bad dreams were happening to which my younger self responded, "in my brain". My mom then explained that if the bad dreams were taking place in my brain, that I am in control of the dream and can do whatever I want in them as a result.

Embracing the idea that I am in control of what I think and feel, I began having fun in those bad dreams. Right before the shark tried to attack me, I would grab it by its nose and throw it a mile away. I could do this because I realized I was in control and I had the power to dictate what was going on in my own domain.

Controlling the volume consists of managing the noise both internally as well as externally. Below, I go into each of them and break down the importance of volume control in all areas. I will detail the benefits and risks connected to understanding and applying the right management approach.

EXTERNAL VOLUME CONTROL

Every day we are overwhelmed by external noises that play a role in our thoughts and actions. This ranges from peer pressure, social media, societal expectations and pressures as well as the media's portrayal of who we are and what is expected of us, family, teachers, and so much more. We are often presented with positive, empowering or inspiring sounds that we want to embrace and welcome.

However, we are also presented with negative and defeating sounds that can lead to harmful thoughts and behavior. This is a major concern for young men due to constant messaging that is presented with ideals and images of what a man looks, thinks and acts like from both good and bad sources. In addition, and arguably more harmful, is the constant representation of young men being uncontrollable and disruptive.

When proper volume control is not in place, and in situations where young men have an audience and are more likely to act for the benefit of others rather than in their own self-interest, the consequences can be severe and long-lasting.

The volume needs to be turned down on any external noise that is harmful, negative or has you questioning your value or worth. The source of this negative noise can be from people you consider friends, people who are your family or those who wish you failure. It can include social media, the music that we listen to, what we consume on television, or the video games that we play.

Turning down the volume does not necessarily mean trying not to listen as hard or minimize how well we listen or hear something. Volume management includes making the conscious decisions to avoid being around certain people or limiting who you share your goals and dreams with. It also includes how you invest your time and the benefits that are associated with that investment.

Positive external sounds need to be welcomed and the volume needs to be jacked up in those situations. The greatest source of this positivity can be found in people within our lives who show unconditional support. These valued supporters will consistently display love and the desire to see us grow and succeed.

Taking in these positive actions and feelings will make us stronger, more empowered and invincible are at the core of personal and professional growth.

Volume management, in this case, means bringing the people who genuinely care about us closer to us and involving them more intentionally in our daily lives. It means consuming as much of that positivity as possible and converting that energy into positive results, thoughts, and actions.

The hard part in external volume control is in identifying whether or not a particular source has an actual or potential influence over us. If I were to ask a person which food they think is healthier to intake between a salad and a hamburger,

I believe the choice can be made easily. Unfortunately, identifying whether or not a person or source is adding or subtracting value from your life can be very challenging.

For example, a close friend who you believe is a positive source may be feeding you negativity and trying to hold you back. On the contrary, a person who is tough on you may feel like a negative source but ultimately, that person truly wants the absolute best for you.

We have to be very mindful and careful of how we identify these external sources and how we react to them. This may require redefining what a friend is, or what family means or how we spend our time. This is all part of maturing and evolving into adulthood and welcoming the potential for success.

INTERNAL VOLUME CONTROL

Managing the volume internally is not only more important than managing the external volume but is fortunately the one aspect of this concept that we are in greater control over. We cannot always control the external noise that is around us, as we cannot always choose our environment. We can, however, control what happens to that noise, and the potential impact and influence it can have, once we hear it.

Positive internal volume control can be empowering and motivating while negative internal volume control can lead to self-defeating and harmful thoughts.

Directly connected to our ability to control our internal volume is in identifying and managing our *self-worth*.

Self-worth is an internal feeling of being good enough and worthy of love from others. It involves loving and valuing yourself independent of external influences such as other people's opinions or how many likes or follows you have on social media. Knowing and appreciating your self- worth not only influences how you view yourself but plays a significant role in how you allow others to influence who you are and how you feel about yourself in other words- managing the external noise.

Understanding and applying this skill is particularly important for a young man who is constantly pressured to act or confirm his behavior in efforts to seek approval or acceptance from others. Being comfortable in your own skin, independent of the opinions of others, is what *self-love* and *self-worth* is all about. This approach gets significantly easier as you get older and realize how little people's opinions of you matter. Soon after recognizing your own self- worth, you won't allow the voices of others to influence your decisions. As a young person, learn to appreciate the challenges of being yourself and acting independently. Trust me- the reward here far outweighs any concerns.

Managing the volume means controlling the messages you allow to play in your head on a daily basis. In good times and bad, through failure or success, whether alone or around a ton of people, learn to hear the sound of your own voice.

Eliminate self-defeating thoughts such as questioning your intelligence, evaluating yourself based on other people or believing that you are not worthy or deserving of happiness, success and greatness. Promote thoughts of empowerment, self-confidence, and belief in your own ability. Be careful with two incredibly important words- "I am," as they have the power to crush and defeat you (ex.- "I am not good enough" or "I am not deserving of love") or they can uplift you within any obstacle or challenge (ex.- "I am unstoppable" or "I am capable of anything I put my mind to").

We control the volume in so many ways in our daily lives for things that are essentially insignificant. Learning to control the volume when it comes to how we care for ourselves and how we remove negativity from our thought process is one of the most powerful ways to manage the volume in our lives.

CHAPTER 7

RESPONSIBILITY AND ACCOUNTABILITY

*"Accept responsibility for your life.
Know that it is you who will get you where
you want to go, no one else."*

– Les Brown

Many young people are in a rush to grow up and become an adult due to many perceived perks associated with adulthood. The ability to drive, access to money and not having to be told what to do (to an extent) are some. While there are certain "advantages" to being an adult, there are just as many if not more new challenges that are presented. One of those challenges is that as you get older, there are more expectations placed on you with excuses become less viable of an option when things do not get done. This is the birth and progression of responsibility and accountability. While these challenges increase with age, it is important to understand and appreciate this progression of mentality at a young age.

Responsibility and accountability are often used interchangeably, as if they were synonyms. The reality is that they are two different concepts that each deserve equal attention, understanding and application as a young man grows into manhood. Considering this, the goal is to break down each concept separately with examples and insight to better understand the importance of each and how to develop both respectively.

DIFFERENCES BETWEEN RESPONSIBILITY AND ACCOUNTABILITY

The difference between responsibility and accountability, in a nutshell, is as follows: you are *responsible* for things but you are *accountable* to people (and yourself) as it relates to those things. As a result, responsibility must come before accountability. For example, if you are asked to babysit your younger sibling then you take on that responsibility and must act accordingly by following the rules and guidelines as laid out by your parent or guardians. If something goes wrong while babysitting then you must be accountable to your parents or guardians for the result. Ultimately, we take responsibility but are held accountable.

There are additional differences between responsibility and accountability that are worth noting in the hopes of better understanding the two concepts. Another key difference is that responsibility can be shared, such as working in a team for example, but accountability is generally held to one person. Another distinction is that we accept responsibility on our own, meaning we make the conscious decision to take on a responsibility. However, once we accept this responsibility we then become accountable to someone else. Regardless of their differences it is important to understand that on the journey to manhood, as well as success, there will inevitable be a combination of the two concepts in play most of the time. Increased responsibility and accountability lead to increased chances of success, growth and marketability as a student, professional and as a brand.

RESPONSIBILITY

Responsibility is a skill and character trait that is developed over time. It is one in which you are fully in control of developing and can ultimately use it to your benefit to make yourself more marketable professionally as well as personally. Responsibility is shaped by the people around us and what we see and experience. We take all those things and they factor into our action and our decisions. This means that responsibility is ultimately a conscious and personal decision and is solely within your control to develop. Ultimately this means that you cannot blame anyone for your mistakes or lack of responsibility.

Responsibility can be developed in several ways. As this is a skill that you are in control of, the ways presented to develop responsibility are all things that you can put into practice independent of any outside factors or people. You can work this skill out daily and it will grow- and it is never too early to start! Developing responsibility means stopping certain bad habits and approaches and replacing them with positive and empowering ones.

AVOID MAKING EXCUSES

If we try hard enough, we can come up with an excuse to justify any failure or shortcoming. Excuses are always around and available. However, in using an excuse we are transferring the blame from ourselves to another person or thing. This is essentially being irresponsible. If you make a mistake, if you fail at something, if you fail to arrive somewhere on time- take ownership of the problem and work to address it moving forward.

AVOID COMPLAINING

People who spend a lot of time complaining invest a lot of time and energy into talking and little to no energy into doing or addressing the problem. If the problem is something that is out of your control (ex.- if it is raining outside) then it is fine to complain but understand no amount of complaining will fix anything so why invest energy in that way. If the problem is something in your control then rather than complaining work towards addressing or fixing the problem. Take responsibility into your own hands and work to invest your energy in solving problems and remaining positive.

AVOID PROCRASTINATING

No one looks forward to doing something they do not enjoy. As a kid I absolutely hated washing the dishes. Here is the problem- if I spent all day coming up with things to do instead of washing the dishes guess what would be waiting for me in the sink at the end of the day? The dirty dishes! The responsible thing to do is to accept what needs to get done and get it done. This is how successful people become successful and maintain success. It is absolutely more fun to watch television or scroll the internet than study or work on a project but think about how responsible that really is and decide it if makes sense. Not everything in life that needs to be done will be fun but responsible people do not let that feeling prevent them from handling the task at hand. Time is something we can never get back so it is important to use it wisely.

AVOID HIDING FROM RESPONSIBILITY

A great way to learn about responsibility, is to grow personally from it, is to take on responsibilities and use those experiences to become more responsible. A harmful way to avoid the pressures of taking on a responsibility and limiting any concern about failure is to avoid taking on any responsibilities. There are a few issues with that. First, avoiding responsibility is almost impossible as you grow into adulthood. We all have to take on responsibilities as we get older and more independent. Second, considering that responsibility is unavoidable, it is impossible to develop that skill by avoiding it. It is like thinking you can better at basketball by not playing the sport at all. Responsibility is like a muscle- the more we use it and work it out the stronger we become and the more responsibility we can handle.

ACCOUNTABILITY

Accountability comes in two forms - internal accountability & external accountability. *Internal accountability* is when you are accountable to yourself, meaning you make sure you keep your promises, stay loyal to your values and beliefs and take ownership of your actions. *External accountability* is when you are accountable to others which impacts how people view and interact with you on a personal and professional level.

Both forms of accountability are essential to understand and grow and both are equally important. Many people tend to focus more time and energy one form over the other, most often external accountability. However, external factors can only influence and guide your behavior so far- it must be matched by an internal sense of accountability to help form a mutually strong overall skill.

For example, let's say I hire you for a position in my company and assign myself as your direct supervisor. In that situation you have external accountability to me. As your supervisor I will be monitoring your work product and ensuring you are doing your job as expected. In a situation where you struggle to get to work on time or fall asleep at your desk because you were up late playing video games, that is no longer an external accountability issue. It falls on you to hold yourself accountable internally. You must ensure that you do what needs to be done to arrive to work on time and to go to sleep early to be well rested for work.

As important a role that external accountability plays in personal and professional growth, I believe the greatest obstacle is understanding and mastering internal accountability. I believe people who are able to hold themselves accountable consistently and effectively are able to think and behave in ways that will lead to greater positive external accountability. Internal accountability helps to develop motivation, passion, and a commitment to personal excellence. This creates an effective and consistent work ethic that produces positive results. There are several ways to promote internal accountability that I have personally found to be empowering.

FOCUS ON YOUR WORK PRODUCT

Taking pride in your work product helps to increase internal accountability. Everything you do, whether as a student or employee, should be something that you take pride in putting your name on and letting people know it is associated with your effort. By taking this perspective it helps to ensure that you hold yourself and the work you produce to a higher level and invest the necessary time and energy to make sure that happens. For example, rather than spending five minutes to complete an essay for class just to get it done, spend as much time as you need so that the finished product is something you are proud of and stand by.

SET GOALS

You can set two types of goals- long-term goals, which you hope to accomplish in a longer period of time such as a few months, and short- term goals, which have shorter deadlines and ultimately help you to accomplish your long-term goals. Setting a goal does not build accountability by itself. The process of working towards, and accomplishing, your goals is where internal accountability is ultimately developed. Staying focused, completing the necessary tasks and making sacrifices as needed are all examples of ways to build internal accountability and greatly help in accomplishing the goals you set.

GET AN ACCOUNTABILITY COACH

An accountability coach is an effective way to use external accountability to promote internal accountability. An accountability coach is someone who regularly touches base with you to see if you are staying on task and working on those goals and assignments that you set out for yourself. It is easy for us to come up with excuses internally but when someone puts us on the spot it feels and sounds much more difficult. For example, if I make a commitment to go to the gym three days a week I can easily decide one day that I am too tired or too lazy to go. However, if I know that I have an accountability coach that will ask me if I went to the gym, and will not accept me being lazy or tired, then I will be forced to step up and handle my commitment. An accountability coach is someone that you trust who will exercise tough love if and when needed. This can be a teacher, a counselor, a trusted friend or essentially any responsible person committed to seeing you succeed!

CHAPTER 8

INTEGRITY

"The greatness of a man is not in how much wealth he acquires, but in his integrity and his ability to affect those around him positively."

– Bob Marley

As someone who loves cars and finds happiness in driving, I find myself behind the wheel of my car at all times of the day and night. My favorite time to drive is late at night because there is less traffic and more open roads. On occasion I find myself in a dilemma while on the road. It would be either very late at night or very early in the morning and I approach a red light on the street. At the light I notice that no one is around for miles- no cars, no pedestrians, no cameras and no police. The dilemma is figuring out what to do- should I run the red light since no one is around and I will likely not get caught or do I follow the rules and stay at the red light until the light turns green? *What would you do under the circumstances?*

What would you do if you have an opportunity to cheat on an exam when the teacher is not looking? Or you find a wallet with money in it and a license but no one is around? Or your parents tell you that you can watch television until a certain time at night but they fell asleep before you? These are all some of many examples of situations that many of us have found ourselves in. The responses to these situations will vary but it will be easy to distinguish those responses based on integrity and good character and those that are not.

Integrity is the quality of being honest and having strong moral principles. It is about doing the right thing even when no one is looking. Why is it important that no one is looking? When someone is looking, especially a person of authority, we will likely do the right thing. The issue is whether we are doing the right thing out of a strong sense of integrity or are we doing the right thing out of fear of getting in trouble. In the example above, if I mentioned there was a police officer parked on the side of the road by the light when I stopped- you would have to wonder if I stopped because I am a man of integrity or if I stopped because I did not want to get pulled over. If you are able to maintain your principles, be honest and act in a good way when no one is watching then you are demonstrating the qualities of a person of integrity.

Maintaining integrity today, and in particular for young men, is incredibly challenging. Society today is very much about being liked, seeking approval from others and conforming to perceived societal norms, even at the sacrifice of integrity. This significantly impacts the decisions made regarding what actions to take in certain situations. Rather than focusing on doing what is right the question considered is "what will other people think". With the sacrifice of integrity comes a willingness to do anything to be popular and liked. Doing the right thing is not as much fun and is not as well received by peers as doing something that is entertaining or capable of going viral on social media. Integrity, as a result, also incorporates doing the right thing even when people are watching and may not find your actions or response cool or popular.

ACTING WITH INTEGRITY

Integrity plays a critical role in character development in all types of environments, from academic spaces such as schools to professional spaces such as workplaces. Regardless of where you find yourself it is important to understand what acting with integrity incorporates and what it looks like. Acting with integrity is not limited to age or location and should be put into practice early and often in order to nurture its growth as you enter new spaces and encounter new opportunities and challenges. Below are some examples of how to act with integrity that we are often face with and are easy to understand and put into practice.

KEEP YOUR PROMISES

Anyone can make a promise but it takes a person of integrity to keep that promise no matter what. When you make a promise you are making a commitment. Sometimes it is not easy to keep that promise but doing everything you can to keep that promise is part of that commitment. In keeping a promise you demonstrate trustworthiness and integrity and people will view you as being dependable. However, if you make a promise and do not keep it then people will have the opposite view- that you are untrustworthy and dishonest. Be careful and mindful of what you promise to do, or intend on promising, because you will be kept to your word.

DON'T GOSSIP

A person who talks behind someone else's back and either shares personal information, lies or makes fun of someone is an example of acting without integrity. Starting or spreading rumors, even when the people you are sharing it with find it entertaining, can cause you to be labeled as someone who is untrustworthy and lacking integrity. This is especially the case when you enter professional workspaces where the opportunities to gossip are similar to being in grade school. The difference is a lack integrity in the workplace can negatively affect your professional growth and your career.

DON'T EXPECT A REWARD

Similar to how a person can act out of integrity to avoid getting in trouble, a person can act out of integrity for the purposes of receiving a reward. The issue in both situations is that it calls into question whether the decision to act with integrity is genuine or based on an external motivation. Doing the right thing is motivation alone. Any benefit that may come from it is a perk but should not be the basis for acting with integrity. We see this often when people find a wallet or money and return it. For some people they think the idea of returning money is crazy. For others, it is seen as an act of integrity, whether a reward is offered for finding the money or not.

BE POLITE... ALWAYS

Being polite is always the right thing to do. It can be shown in many ways such as saying thank you, holding the door open for someone or sharing something with someone in need. The real challenge with being polite is when the person you are dealing with is being rude or unpolite. A person who chooses to act rude to you should not affect your morals and ethics and get you to act in a way contrary to your integrity. Michelle Obama said it best- "when they go low, we go high". Maintain your high standards of good character and integrity when confronted with rudeness and do not sacrifice who you are and your morals to meet someone on a level beneath you.

HONESTY IS KEY

At the core of integrity is honesty. Being honest is always the best route, even when honesty is not in our best interest. It is easier to tell the truth than it is to lie and keep lying to maintain the original lie.

73

It is also important to note that being honest is not an excuse to be mean or rude either. Maintaining respect, even when being honest about things that may not be pleasant, is always important. Use discretion in terms of when and how to be honest but always remember that honesty is the best policy.

APOLOGIZE WHEN NECESSARY

No one likes to be wrong and it feels like torture to admit or acknowledge when you wrong. However, being able to identify when you are wrong and apologizing when necessary is an important aspect of integrity. Apologizing is not a sign of weakness and it does not make you less of a person or a man. If anything, it is the opposite- it takes a mature and strong person to acknowledge fault, take ownership of it and apologize for it. This is what integrity is all about!

STAND UP FOR WHAT IS RIGHT

A person acting with integrity will stand up for what is right and fair in all situations. This is the reason why I wanted to be a lawyer- I have a passion for fighting for what is right and calling out things that are wrong. Sometimes standing up for what is right comes at the risk of being persecuted or ridiculed. We have seen this throughout history with people like Rosa Parks, who took a stand on injustice by sitting on an area of a bus marked "for white people only" during Jim Crow. When you have morals and beliefs that you are passionate about the need to stand up and fight for them outweighs whether it is the popular opinion. Stand for what you believe in and fight for what is right!

CHAPTER 9

BE A GENTLEMAN

*"A gentleman is one who puts more
into the world than he takes out."*

–George Bernard Shaw

The term "gentleman" brings to mind so many images and descriptions based on my experience and what is often presented in media. I envision a well-dressed, well-spoken, highly respected and intellectual man with a calm demeanor but also someone who is not afraid to fight for what he believes in. While this is often the image of a gentleman, the reality is that being a gentleman is a lifestyle and not just an image. It is not just about looking the part or people making assumptions based on how you present yourself. Being a gentleman is demonstrated in your actions and intentions.

Many of the characteristics and qualities of a gentleman's lifestyle have been, and will be, covered throughout this book- integrity, honesty, hard work, accountability and more. In this chapter I want to focus on some of the smaller actions that may be overlooked or disregarded as part of the lifestyle but are essential parts of it. It is often the small things that carry the most weight when it comes to being a gentleman.

MAINTAIN SOLID EYE CONTACT

Eye contact might be one of the most important forms of non-verbal communication that there is. We draw a lot of assumptions about a person we are communicating with based on eye contact. If a person avoids eye contact we can assume the person is either shy or has something to hide. If a person is staring at the wall while speaking with you it is safe to assume the person is likely not paying attention. An angry stare or scowl can indicate that the person is upset about something. These assumptions are not concrete but are meant to show that everyone makes assumptions based on our non-verbal communication so we have to factor that in when using eye contact and communicating with someone. Direct eye contact indicates that you are paying attention to the speaker and listening, not just hearing, what is being said.

Direct eye contact also leads to other positive assumptions that are vital for effective communication skills. It is seen as being respectful to maintain eye contact as it shows you are giving the speaker your undivided attention. By doing this you are also letting the speaker know that you appreciate their importance which leads to the development of stronger bonds, stronger relationships and trust. In addition, direct eye contact is a sign of confidence in yourself and in what is being communicated. It is a way of letting the person know that you believe in yourself while acknowledging the other person's importance as well.

It is important to note that eye contact, and the assumptions we draw as a result of it, is not and should not be set in stone. One of the main reasons why this is the case is that eye contact can vary based on culture. In general, Western cultures tend to value the presence of eye contact while Eastern ones tend to see eye contact as a form of disrespect. The key to communication is adaptation. Read the situation and the responses by individuals you are speaking with and adapt accordingly. It is also important to be mindful of different perspectives and mentalities connected with eye contact and do not automatically assume that a lack of it means the person was not interested in you or what you had to say.

There is an artform to maintaining direct eye contact, something I was taught by a mentor in college which really changed how I communicated with people. The goal in direct eye contact is to find the line between "I am paying attention to you because I value your importance" and making the person feel uncomfortable or staring. I was taught the 50/80 rule for direct eye contact. When speaking, try to maintain eye contact 50% of the time and when listening try to maintain eye contact for 80% of the time. You can maintain eye contact for a few seconds then subtly look away for a few seconds before returning to eye contact. Try to avoid looking at your watch or at the ceiling or floor to avoid sending a negative assumption- I tend to look generally at the surrounding environment. While this may seem like a lot to remember, as with all other skills it takes practice. The more you practice, and the more you get comfortable with direct eye contact, the better your communication will be.

MASTER THE HANDSHAKE

Another critical non-verbal communication method that can speak volumes about who you are is the handshake. The importance of the handshake goes back many years and has always been symbolic of mutual agreement and respect. The absolute need for men to possess the ability to execute a proper professional handshake is key. I acknowledge in the time of COVID people are reluctant to want to shake hands but this will not always be the case. It is always better to stay ready than to get ready when the time comes to shake hands.

In order to understand the importance of handshakes you must understand the psychology behind it. The person with whom you are shaking hands with can and will make judgments about your character and personality based on how you deliver a handshake. These judgments from a handshake can range from a sense of confidence, importance, and friendliness to arrogance and overconfidence. Those judgments can also include weakness, indifference and insecurity. The proper handshake at the start or end of an encounter can ultimately set the tone of a

Meeting or ensure that you will receive a communication following the meeting.

Similar to eye contact, it is important to consider cultural boundaries and interpretations connected with handshakes. Through experience you will learn that not everyone is comfortable with shaking hands, for reasons not just limited to COVID. Over the years I have attended numerous professional networking events. One time I remember I approached a group of individuals and began shaking everyone's hand while introducing myself. One person in the circle did not extend their hand for a handshake. While I was surprised, and honestly felt a little offended initially, I had to adapt and kept shaking hands. I later found out for that for cultural reasons that person was not comfortable shaking my hand. I am thankful I did not respond negatively and implore others to show the same level of restraint and adaptive skills if ever placed in a similar situation.

In delivering a proper handshake there are several key factors that also play a role. First, you must always be prepared to deliver a handshake in any setting. That means ensuring that your right hand is always free to shake someone's hand. Transitioning anything from your right hand to your left hand should take place before the opportunity to shake hands to avoid any awkward delays. Second, you must consider your body language. If seated, always stand and face the person with whom you are about to shake hands. Eye contact is key here. In addition, avoid having your hands in your pockets, as having your hands out and ready to shake demonstrates an invitation to shake hands while also conveying openness and friendliness. Lastly, you must be aware of what your hands are doing both during and after the handshake. Your hand should be approaching a handshake perpendicular (90-degree angle from the floor) with the goal of making direct and firm contact. Wrap your fingers around the other person's hand as if you were giving their hand a hug. Once contact is made it is customary to squeeze firmly, matching the same level of squeeze as the other person but not squeezing too hard. Pump the handshake up and down 2-3 times, shaking from your elbow as opposed to your wrist. Once the hands are released you take a step back. While there is so much to consider in shaking hands it is important to get in a lot of practice so it becomes second nature and you do not have to think or worry about what to do or not do. With enough practice you will start hearing those compliments like "nice handshake", which is always a step in the right direction.

RESPECT AND DEFEND WOMEN

An important part of a gentleman lifestyle is how we interact with and treat women. This is not just limited to the ladies and women in your family but includes any young lady or woman that you interact with. Sadly, this aspect of the gentleman lifestyle faces the greatest attacks, as many parts of society embraces treating women with disrespect, undermining their value and viewing them as objects rather than people. At the same time, it is important to understand the goal is not to view ladies and women as helpless creatures that need your protection to survive. As gentlemen, it is our responsibility to break these trends and to respect and protect women as people and as equals.

Respecting women takes many forms and includes things that should absolutely be done as well as things to avoid doing. The way in which you speak with ladies and women is a great place to start. Talk to them with respect and avoid name-calling or degrading and disrespectful slurs or names. Refer to the lady or woman by her name and not a nickname or joke name (unless she approves). Avoid referring to ladies and women as "females", as this is disrespectfully diminishing their role and importance by referring to them simply as a gender. Keep your hands to yourself and do not treat ladies and women like one of your "boys" by playfighting or hitting them. In addition, do not touch a lady or woman in any inappropriate way unless you get express permission to do so. It is also important to mind your manners around ladies and women. This means anything that can be perceived as being rude (ex.- cursing at them, burping, etc.). Instead practice being polite, kind and courteous. Small things like offering your seat if there are no options or offering to help go a long way in showing respect. Lastly, in acting with integrity, you should call out your male friends for acting in a way that is disrespectful towards women. We must hold each other accountable as men and gentlemen to ensure that we embrace a mentality of respect towards women.

The "kindergarten rule" is a concept I have been familiar with for a very long time. It basically means that when a boy likes a girl it is easy to tell because the boy harasses, teases, hits or bothers the girl as a form of affection. I am not sure how welcomed this approach is at that young age but I can assure you that as you get older, and women are more aware of what respect looks and feels like, the kindergarten rule should be abandoned completely and replaced with these principles of a gentleman lifestyle.

DEMONSTRATE GOOD SPORTSMANSHIP

Most young men find themselves in some form of competition- it can be sports, video games, board games or many other things. There is no question that the goal in participating in these activities is to win. The reality is that not everyone can win at all things and at all times. The reality is that one of life's greatest lessons can be learned regardless of a win or loss- good sportsmanship. Part of being a gentleman is learning how to win and lose graciously knowing that on any given day we can fall on the win side or the loss side. The way in which we react in either scenario determines if we are following the principles of good sportsmanship.

Good sportsmanship consists of some basic principles that should be understood and applied. In the event that you win, it is important to remain humble and accept the victory with grace. Today is your day but you can easily lose tomorrow. In the event that you lose, don't be a sore loser and come up with excuses or start blaming people or factors outside of your control. Whether you win or lose there are always lessons to be learned- invest time in figuring out how you won so you can repeat it as well as why you lost so you can address it moving forward, provided it is within your control. If you are playing a team sport you must treat everyone on your team with respect and not ridicule or criticize a player for making a mistake. You are in control of your actions so your goal and focus should be on doing your best. Lastly, play fair. Winning is not everything and you should not be willing to sacrifice your morals and principles just for a win.

Every year for over a decade I have hosted debate competitions for elementary, middle and high school students. With competitions come trophies. Before I start the trophy ceremony I give the same speech each year. Regardless of who wins a trophy, the fact that the students showed up, pushed beyond their comfort zone, engaged in good sportsmanship and tried their best then that means every participant is a winner. A trophy looks great as a prize but the true reward comes in the skills developed in competing as well as in taking on a challenge and pushing yourself to the limit.

BE EMPATHETIC

With all the madness in the world, from fighting to disagreements, there is no simple solution to bringing about an end to it all and fostering a greater sense of community. One key skill that I believe can go a long way in uniting people is empathy. Humans are by nature self- centered creatures- we view the world from a very subjective perspective that is focused on our views, our feelings and our experiences. Empathy is a skill that allows us to view situations and scenarios, as best as possible, from the perspective of someone else in the hopes of increasing understanding and potentially resolving conflict.

Empathy is the ability to understand and share the feelings of other people by placing yourself in their shoes and viewing the situation from their perspective. For example, I may call a friend short and not take it seriously because I know it is a joke and not meant to be harmful. However, empathy would allow me to see how it may feel to be called short from the perspective of my friend to better help me understand if and how it can be hurtful. Empathy is important in that it allows us, and in some cases forces us, to realize that there are multiple perspectives to a situation and what we think and feel may not be what someone else thinks and feels. This has a direct impact in our actions and what we say, being careful to consider the feelings of others before doing and saying things.

I often argue that empathy is tied into consequential thinking. Consequential thinking involves thinking about and evaluating the consequences of your actions before acting and evaluating what actions to take, if any. Empathy is similar in that if we get into the habit of viewing situations from other people's perspectives it can, and should, affect what we say and how we say it. Can you imagine how different this world would look like if we considered other people's feelings before we spoke or acted?

In a world where many say chivalry, a medieval system associated with courteous and moral knights, is dead, I am hopeful that the young men reading this book can grow in to strong, capable men who have learned respect, generosity and confidence.

CHAPTER 10

ASK FOR HELP

*"Asking for help is never a sign of weakness. It's one of the bravest things you can do.
And it can save your life!"*

– Lily Collins

Asking others for help is both an essential foundation of success and growth as well as a source of anxiety and fear for many people. Every successful person has, at some point, received help in some form or fashion. It can be in the form of advice, feedback or guidance involving a challenging situation. Asking for help, with all the amazing positives that can result from doing so, also instills fear in people. There are a lot of negative assumptions and fears associated with asking for help that often prevent people from doing so.

Here are a few of the more popular reasons/misconceptions why people, including myself, have used to justify not asking for help when needed-

IT IS A SIGN OF WEAKNESS

Somehow asking for help has been associated with being weak or inferior. Particularly among men this is a popular misconception, as men are expected to have the answers or be able to figure it out without needing assistance. The reality is that asking for help is a sign of strength rather than weakness. The ability to identify when there is a need or deficit in your capabilities or understanding and seeking support is a tremendous skill to have and use. It is a demonstration of your intelligence and strength.

I CAN HANDLE IT ON MY OWN / DON'T NEED HELP

This has been my greatest barrier to asking for help- allowing my pride to get in the way of me acknowledging that I can't figure it out and it would be easier and more efficient to ask for help. I respect when people push to work things out and try to work towards a solution. That level of resilience is truly admirable. However, there is a point where you have to acknowledge that you have reached the extent of your abilities as it relates to the matter. Convincing yourself that you do not need help when in fact you do is ultimately a waste of your time and energy and will just make the work even harder, and longer, to handle.

DON'T WANT TO BOTHER OTHER PEOPLE WITH MY PROBLEMS

One of the last things we want is to be a burden or a problem to other people. We convince ourselves that by talking to people about our problems and asking for help that we are a nuisance. By doing so, however, we are taking away the opportunity for people who truly and genuinely care about us to support and help us. In addition, we often do not know what other people are dealing with and by opening up about your problems and asking for help you are helping them to do the same.

Just as important as what and when to ask for help is who to ask for help. Keep in mind to be careful of who you ask for help because a bad experience from the wrong person will impact your willingness to ask someone else for help. Those people in your life who have demonstrated a genuine and unconditional level of support and love towards you are the best people to seek help from. This includes people who you talk to regularly and who genuinely listen to you rather than hear you and wait for an opportunity to talk about themselves. There are no "automatics' on this list- not all family fall into this category, not all friends fall into this category and not every adult in your life falls into this category. The art and skill of identifying those people in your lives that are sources of empowerment, support and strength should be now, and will absolutely become one of the most important skills you can develop and master.

HOW TO ASK FOR HELP

I never really understood that there was a right way and a wrong way to ask for help until I became someone who people come to for help and support. I quickly realized that many people, including myself, asked for help the wrong way and it significantly impacted the response. There is a process that I have come to understand which significantly increases the chances of receiving impactful and meaningful help and also builds confidence in your ability to understand and structure the obstacles that we are facing.

BE SPECIFIC ABOUT THE HELP YOU NEED (& WHY)

Before you approach anyone to ask for help, you should have a script prepared. The goal of this script is to ensure that you are clear, concise and direct in explaining your situation, why you need help, what specific help you need and how that person is in a position to provide that help. This is also very helpful in understanding your own needs and how to articulate them. It is incredibly frustrating to be approached for help and either not understand what help is needed, why I am being asked or have to hear details that are not relevant to the help being sought. Keep your request simple and straight forward to avoid any confusion and significantly increase the odds of getting the help needed.

SKIP THE ELECTRONICS

With the increase in technology usage, come numerous ways to interact with people. I am not sure if it is because I am old school but I always prefer, and advise others, that personal and in- person communication should always be the preferred method of communication, within reason of course.

There are certain things that an electronic communication cannot convey that an in-person or even a call can- enthusiasm, energy, personal connection and so much more. In addition, think of how many other things you have going on while texting or on your phone? Your attention and energy are not fully invested in the conversation. When in-person, the focus and energy is invested in the conversation and the distractions are significantly limited. Lastly, I always suggest for people to find ways to separate themselves from everyone else to stand out for positive reasons. One way to stand out is to ask for an in-person meeting while everyone else is e-mailing or sending a text. It is in the small ways that we can make a huge impact.

FOLLOW-UP

Let's say that you approach someone with a clear and concise need during an in-person conversation and that person helps you out in the way you need. This does not mark the end of the relationship simply because you got what you wanted. The next important step is to keep that person updated on your progress following the help provided. Did the support help? Did it lead to new issues? Do you need additional support? If a person takes the time to help you it means they are invested in your success. That investment goes beyond just giving help but also finding out what happened after receiving the help. In addition, if this is someone you trust enough to approach in the first place for help you do not want to lose or harm that relationship.

Regular follow- up conversations reinforce the relationship and makes it more likely that the person will be willing to help you again in the future.

MENTAL HEALTH AND COUNSELING

Asking for help goes well beyond help on your homework or on completing a project. Help is not limited to schoolwork or related but also includes your social and emotional growth. It has been a very challenging few years and for many people the true impact of these challenges may not have really registered in people. Many people may be dealing with personal issues and not know what is wrong, who to turn to for support or how to ask for help. Asking for help from an emotional and psychological standpoint for young men and men is particularly difficult and there is a negative false stigma associated with it. The importance of mental health does not diminish based on gender or age. Counseling and therapy, whether with a clinical professional or a school guidance counselor, is necessary maintenance and something no one should be ashamed of asking for help for.

It is critical to remember that things do not have to be going wrong for you to seek help. For example, I own an older car that has a reputation in the car community as both an absolute beast but also one with a lot of mechanical issues. I am often approached by people who ask me about my car, specifically how I manage the mechanical issues the car is notoriously known for. I explain that in the years I have owned the vehicle I have never had any issues or surprises related to the mechanics. The shocked look by many people is often followed up by a question related to how I have been able to avoid any issues. My response is simple- I do not wait for things to break in order to replace or fix it. I engage in preventive work by maintaining and fixing things before they break so the car stays stronger. Similar to my car, I engage in the same approach when it comes to my mental health. Counseling occurs in the good and bad times so I am better able to handle both when they happen at random times.

Asking for help from an emotional standpoint does not need to happen when things are wrong or we feel the world is falling apart. We must do preventative maintenance as well. We cannot control life or what happens to us so it is always better to stay ready than to get ready when things go wrong. Asking for help is strategic as much as it is helpful.

CHAPTER 11

EMOTIONAL INTELLIGENCE

"I don't want to be at the mercy of my emotions. I want to use them, to enjoy them, and to dominate them."

— Oscar Wilde

Emotional intelligence is one of the most important skills to understand on a personal and professional basis. Our emotions play a role, often a significant one, in our thought process, our actions and our perspective.

Navigating and understanding our emotions is challenging enough and only gets more complicated when we are consistently placed in situations where we interact with people who also have emotions and are trying to navigate and understand them.

Emotional intelligence is a significant challenge for young boys and young men who, based on brain development, are not able to fully engage in consequential thinking and impulse control. Behavior that is impulsive and driven by emotions are often very harmful and can have serious consequences.

Emotional intelligence affects how we manage our behavior, navigate through complex social situations, and guide us as we aim to make decisions that will lead to positive results. Essentially it consists of two major aspects: (1) understanding and managing your own emotions, or the personal aspect; and (2) understanding and navigating through the emotions of other people, or the social aspect. While both aspects present challenges, it is much easier to understand your emotions, how your emotions affect how you think and also how you act. In dealing with the emotions of other people it is more about how you respond to other people's emotions and how it affects your actions.

An example of the personal aspect of emotional intelligence is when I am "hangry" (angry as a result of being hungry). I know when I am "hangry" that I am irritable and easily annoyed. During these moments I make a conscious decision to avoid interacting with people as much as possible so that I do not take out my frustration at being hungry on people who have nothing to do with my hunger. An example of the social aspect of emotional intelligence I experience a lot is when people are upset due to the weather (i.e. it is raining, snowing, too hot or too cold). When a person upset at the weather approaches me and projects their anger or frustration onto me I know I have several options in terms of how to respond- some good and some bad. Exercising emotional intelligence is recognizing that I am not the reason why the person is upset as I do not control the weather. In that situation I would avoid escalating the situation but instead acknowledge they are upset and wish them the best in dealing with it.

Below are some of the signs of emotional intelligence that have been identified by adult professional men as being among the most critical for young boys to apply:

EMOTIONAL CONTROL

One of my favorite reminders from a friend is to never make permanent decisions based on temporary emotions. This concept ties directly in with consequential thinking, which is considering the consequences of your actions before acting. It is critical to think and plan before acting or responding, especially when emotions are involved. Also recognize that the immediate response that you think may feel good can potentially have long term negative consequences (ex. - someone bumps into you and you decide to push the person instead of excuse it and end up in trouble).

AUTHENTICITY

Say what you mean, mean what you say, stand by your principles and values and do not compromise your individuality. The truth is that everyone is not going to like who you are or what you have to say and that is a part of life. This should not deter you from being genuine and honest about who you are. Do not sacrifice who you are or try to define yourself in a way that makes other people happy.

The thing that makes you so incredibly valuable in this world is that there is only one of you. Don't give that up for anyone.

EMPATHY

Showing empathy involves understanding other people's feelings and thoughts. It is exercised by placing yourself in the "shoes" of the other person and attempting to understand their position. In doing so you are not as quick to assume or judge a person. You do not have to agree with the other person's position but you can grow a greater understanding of it, which can play a huge role in how you interact and connect with other people.

SUPPORTIVE OF OTHERS

A true sign of emotional intelligence, and leadership, is when someone is able to encourage and motivate others to become the best version of themselves. I tell people all the time that we can all work together and we can all win- we do not have to sabotage each other or wish failure. Compliment others on their performance. Acknowledge hard work and successes in others. Show appreciation for dedication and applaud achievements. Emotional intelligence is relevant here because this skill involves placing others ahead of yourself. This can be challenging but rewarding for all parties involved.

STAYING COMMITTED / RESILIENCE

Your ability to stay committed to seeing a task through despite how difficult or challenging it may be demonstrates a high level of emotional intelligence. It will always be easier to quit, especially when times get difficult or a more interesting distraction presents itself. Consistently staying committed speaks to your reliability and trustworthiness as a person.

MOOD MANAGEMENT

We cannot control what happens to us but we can control how we react to it and how we allow it to affect us. We are in control of our emotions and can make conscious decisions about what we think and feel and how we let that impact how we act. For example, if you wake up and accept the idea that you will have a bad day then this will play a significant role in your emotions and how you interact with other people. However, if you wake up and accept the idea that you will have a great day then your emotions will follow suit and it will positively impact your thoughts and actions.

As young men prepare for future employment and careers, it is important to note that emotional intelligence is one of the most sought-after skills by employers. As most jobs involve working with other people, whether it be co-workers or clients, the ability to utilize and navigate emotions can lead to great success and growth.

CHAPTER 12

PERSONAL BRANDING

"Personal branding is about managing your name — even if you don't own a business."

– Tim Ferris

Branding is everywhere. We are inundated with branding at every turn- from clothing, cars, restaurants and so much more. We are so familiar with brands and logos that we can identify these brands from a mile away. We have placed personal value and worth to these brands. We make conscious and sub-conscious decisions about what to buy or where to eat or where to go based on the packaging and marketing of these brands. While the concept and practice of branding has long been associated with businesses and companies, personal branding is important for each person looking to be successful as an individual.

Personal branding is the practice of marketing yourself as a brand. Think about yourself as the CEO of the most important business there is- You, Inc. You are responsible for the characteristics associated with this brand, what the brand stands for and you must also provide incentives for people to want to support and trust your brand. One of the best ways to start is with your personal story. Who are you? What are you about? What drives you as a person? What are your goals, dreams and aspirations? What do you bring to the table and how can you help others? All of this information goes towards defining your brand. The best part is that the passion and energy will easily follow, as you are building something off of someone you know better than anyone else in the world- YOU!

A mentality I have often hear from young people related to resisting the concept of personal branding is that they don't care about what people think about them. To be clear, being comfortable in your own skin independent of what anyone else thinks about you is a true superpower. In life, not everyone will like you, even if you are the nicest and most caring person in the history of time. Being true to yourself and genuine is more important than everyone liking you. However, when it comes to personal branding it works a little differently. Personal branding is about promoting the qualities and characteristics about yourself that you want people to know and ultimately invest time and energy in supporting and networking with. Nike's approach is not about worrying if people like their brand or not. It is about drawing new customers and keeping previous customers connected and interested. Similar to Nike, your goal does not have to be to get everyone to like you or to change who you are to appease other people but it should be to be the best version of yourself so others will want to connect with you and help you grow and evolve.

ONLINE V. OFFLINE BRANDING

Personal branding essentially lives in two areas- the online brand and the offline brand. Your online brand is most effective at extending your brand to people and avenues that you may otherwise not have access to. Sharing stories and testimonials or posting professional photos of you will amplify your brand and reach new audiences while growing support in existing audiences. Offline branding will strengthen the connections and relationships that you have made with people in-person over the course of living life. This ranges from friends, educators, people in your community and so many more people who you regularly interact with daily. Your reputation and brand in person will develop and strengthen in- person relationships and also open doors to new opportunities as well as grow your online presence.

Personal branding starts offline. Whether you know it or not, you already have a brand, whether it is a positive one or a negative one. Your character, integrity and reputation all encompass your personal brand. Your brand includes how you dress, how you interact with people and how you carry yourself in different situations. It is about your level of trust, your honesty, and your values. If you really think about it, this entire book is about developing your brand. The great thing about personal branding is that you are completely in control. Every day you have an opportunity to control your brand in every interaction. One way to gauge your offline brand is to ask yourself "what do people say about me when I am not in the room?". If you feel people speak highly of you then you likely have a good brand. If, however, you feel people will speak negatively of you in terms of your characteristics or behavior then you need to focus on rebranding yourself.

Online branding is the more challenging aspect of personal branding, primarily because most people use social media in a way that is harmful to their brand than helpful. Making threatening or inappropriate comments, sharing disrespectful pictures or engaging in cyberbullying or name-calling all contribute to a negative and harmful online brand. Many people believe that as long as their offline brand is positive, and their online presence is private then they are in good shape. The reality is there is no such thing as privacy when it comes to the internet and social media and anyone who is competent on using computers can discover the things you want to keep hidden, such as your social media. In fact, most college admission officers, scholarship providers and employers engage in an online search of applicants to verify if the persons offline presence matches their online presence. It is essential not only to maintain a positive and inspiring overall personal brand but to ensure that it is equally shown both offline as well as online.

Below are two of the most important reasons why personal branding is so important. Keep in mind that it is never too early to start personal branding and, while the core principles remain the same, it will grow significantly more important as you enter the professional world.

BUILDS TRUST – the reason why people spend hours waiting online to buy a phone or spend hundreds of dollars to buy a pair of sneakers is because of the trust they have in the brand. People are willing to do whatever possible to be a part of the brand and support the products the brand creates. By creating a positive personal brand you can also influence people's trust in you and drive them to want to support you.

BUILDS CONFIDENCE – while discovering your strengths and positive qualities and working to showcase them you build confidence in yourself and your abilities. As more people entrust you and are drawn to you based on your personal brand it will also increase your confidence. The more confident you are in yourself and your abilities the more amazing things you do which will help to grow your personal brand. It is an amazing cycle of growth and development of self-worth.

SOCIAL MEDIA USE

It is important to mention the use of social media in general in addition to how it plays into online branding. A critical thing to keep in mind as it relates to social media is that there is no expectation of privacy. This means that as much as you may believe the things you post on social media are private, in actuality, they are not.

Your images can be found independent of your account and your views can be widely shared without even being accepted as a friend or follower. This is very important to note as college admission officers, scholarship providers, employers, and many more key people use basic Google searches to discover if your online brand matches the information provided on your resume or personal statement. Be incredibly mindful of what you post and the information you share, as it can be very harmful to your brand and may negatively impact potential positive opportunities.

On the flip side, you can use the information provided to your advantage when it comes to branding. If you know that there is a focus on ensuring your online brand matches your offline brand, make every effort to create a solid and consistent brand across the board. Use your social media to highlight positive and empowering things about yourself for people to see when they search you. Create a LinkedIn account (if you meet the age requirements) which is a social media platform for professionals to network and connect. Your social media account can be a digital resume that puts into color the well-rounded and successful individual you are.

A personal brand isn't just a logo or cool fonts. Your personal brand is what you show and tell people about who you are and what values are important to you. Create, build and promote a personal brand that will make people want to wait in line for hours or go out of their way to be a part of and support.

CHAPTER 13

SELF MOTIVATION

*"Don't downgrade your dream just to fit your reality-
upgrade your conviction to match your destiny."*

– Stuart Scott

Think of a goal that you are working towards right now. It can be personal, professional or academic. Why have you not achieved that goal yet?

The responses will vary but most will involve some type of external factor- either you do not have enough time, don't have the skills or knowledge to achieve the goal, or you don't have the money to make the goal happen. While these factors may play a role behind why you have not accomplished your goal, the reality is that it all comes down to self-motivation. A person, regardless of the factors presented before them, can make any goal a reality if that person is driven and focused enough to make it happen. This is at the core of self-motivation and is what leads to success.

Self-motivation involves finding the ability to do whatever needs to get done to achieve progress on a goal without relying on or being influenced by external factors. It means tapping into the internal hunger, passion and desire to grow and succeed and using that as fuel to drive you through pain, fear or external obstacles that may try to stop or slow you down. One of the greatest examples that I have ever witnessed of self-motivation was Michael Jordan playing in the 1997 NBA Finals. Despite suffering from flu-like symptoms, dehydration and exhaustion, Jordan scored 38 points to help his team win the game. His will-power and passion resulted in one of the greatest single player performances in the history of the NBA Finals. If he lost or didn't play well could anyone blame him? I am sure we would agree he had a valid reason to justify if that was the case. However, Michael Jordan was not willing to accept any excuses and showcased a level of determination that is truly admirable.

Due to the fact that self-motivation is a very personal and subjective equation to figure out, not every approach will work for everyone. We must each individually find what motivates us and keeps us pushing forward, keeping in mind that the answer may change repeatedly over time.

TAKE RESPONSIBILITY OVER YOUR LIFE

There should be no one more motivated to see your success, your happiness and your growth than you. As a result you need to make the decisions, and sometimes they are difficult, that will place you in a better position to achieve those rewards. There are challenges, risks and rewards from being the captain of your own ship. The challenge is that you are in control of the decisions you make and you need to make sure you remain motivated to push forward when faced with adversity or challenges. The reward is that you get to take most, if not all, of the credit for the decisions and actions it took to achieve that success. The risk is you have no one to blame for any failures when you are in charge. Taking these factors into account, it is important to realize that you need to take control of your life and actively and daily work towards going down the path you want for yourself.

WHAT IS YOUR WHY?

At first glance this seems like a very odd question to ask or be asked. By figuring out your why, you are really trying to dig deep and figure out what motives you. What is the compelling reason or purpose behind what you want to accomplish? The answer to your why is very personal but should be something so strong and meaningful that it outweighs any thoughts of quitting or giving in to external challenges. When you connect your goals to your why you will always remain self- motivated. This is the basis for the saying "when you love what you do for a living, you will never work a day in your life".

While I cannot define your why, I strongly advise against making your why based on material things, especially money. Let's just say that your why is making money. If you made $500, will you be satisfied? What about $5,000? Or $500,000?

When money is your why, you run the risk of never feeling fulfilled or happy because there is always more money to be made and money alone is not going to lead to a sense of fulfillment. Your why should be something significantly more meaningful and personal for you.

USE THE RIGHT WORDS

Language plays a powerful role in our perception and connection with self-motivation and working towards goals. When you use words that are not decisive and clear you can often find yourself unmotivated and without focus. For example, when we use the word "want" when describing a goal. When we want to do something it is not definitive. It does not mean that we will actually do it but instead just shows an interest in wanting to do it. In my opinion, this is where most people fall short of staying motivated. Now switch out "want" with "must" and the focus and energy changes. Now it is no longer an interest but a commitment. Describe your goals as musts and not wants and your ability to stay motivated to see it through, despite obstacles, will significantly increase.

In addition to how we form our goals, we also have to be mindful of the way we talk to ourselves. It is completely normal to talk to yourself- whether it is to hype yourself up, provide words of encouragement or celebrate an accomplishment. This is a powerful way to maintain your focus and passion on a task. However, it is also important to avoid using harmful or self-defeating words. For example, describing yourself as a failure or saying to yourself that you are not good enough or worthy will have a significant impact on your outlook and will negatively affect your ability to achieve goals. This is why most successful people start their day with a positive affirmation to prepare whatever challenges life has that day (ex.- "I am going to have an amazing day" or "I will accomplish all of my goals for the day").

VISUALIZE SUCCESS

Visualization, the practice of imagining what you want to achieve, is a powerful tool that I learned during an unlikely time. I have played pool, or billiards, for many years. I would often compete in leagues or tournaments where the stress of every shot could be felt.

One of the issues I struggled with playing pool was I would often worry about what would go wrong, such as missing a shot or losing a match. By investing energy in the negative I basically made it a reality. A good friend of mine taught me about using visualization in a positive way. Rather than invest energy on what I do not want to happen what I began to do was close my eyes and envision things going the way that I wanted. I would see me taking the perfect shot and the ball going into the pocket. Once I opened my eyes it was just a matter of taking and making the shot that I already made in my head.

A great way to stay motivated is to see and feel what it will be like when you succeed. Visualize yourself winning that award or making the shot or getting that great score on your exam. Try to connect with how amazing that feeling would be to be in that position. When you open your eyes you should be motivated to make that vision a reality. The motivation is not just seeing yourself in real life accomplishing that task but also feeling that amazing feeling as well.

BE YOUR OWN CHEERLEADER

Let's be honest- it feels amazing when someone compliments, praises or acknowledges your hard work or success. It is such an awesome feeling knowing other people can identify something great in you. The issue is that we can easily place ourselves in a situation where we rely on other people to compliment and praise us, which can put you in a position where you are constantly seeking validation from other people. Rather than waiting for, or seeking, praise from others, be your own cheerleader. This can take shape in many ways-compliment yourself, praise yourself, give yourself a high five. Do not rely on anyone else to recognize your greatness but instead make it a regular habit of doing so yourself.

AVOID COMPARABLE SUCCESS

Similar to the concept that you do not need anyone else to validate your greatness, you should also not base your success or accomplishments on what other people are doing. Everyone operates at their own pace and possess their own skills. Not everyone will progress at the same pace and that should not be used as an indication that something is wrong but just verifies that things are different for different people. As you define success, you define the path to that success and it should not be defined or based on anyone else. Otherwise you will end up focusing energy trying to be a copy of someone else. You are meant to be one of a kind!

CHAPTER 14

BASIC FINANCIAL LITERACY

"The single biggest difference between financial success and financial failure is how well you manage your money. It's simple: to master money, you must manage money."

– T. Harv Eker

Financial literacy is one of the most essential skills growing into adulthood that is taken for granted and overlooked in most educational settings.

The goal of many young people is to make money yet the conversation about how to obtain that money and what to do with that money once obtained is not happening enough. Financial literacy should be a process that is taught at childhood and continued through adulthood. The issue seems to be that many people assume that money management is something that will come with time. The problem is that by the time it is learned it may be too late and a person can be in a very bad financial situation. That was my problem.

I was never formally taught about financial literacy. I always understood the importance of hard work and I definitely enjoyed making money. The issue came once I made money and had to figure out what to do with it. For me, it was easy- spend it on stuff I want. Then I got introduced to a truly dangerous new toy - credit cards. Before I knew it, I was graduating college with thousands of dollars in debt having no clue what I spent the money on.

It was after graduating that I sat down and started to learn about money, credit cards, debt management and how to pay off debt. Now I teach as many people, especially young people, the importance of financial literacy. It does not have to be a scary or complicated topic but is actually very basic and the practice and understanding grows in time.

Why discuss financial literacy in a book targeting young men? The truth is that I have learned through my personal experiences and in learning from the experiences of others that men in particular struggle with money management more so than financial literacy. Generally speaking, men tend to want to be flashy in purchases, focus on spending money on things they want over what they need and fail to properly save money or develop good money management skills. This chapter is arguably one of the most important chapters that, if understood and followed, can lead to tremendous financial independence and increase the chances of creating wealth.

As mentioned, financial literacy can be very complicated but my approach is to keep it very simple and straightforward. I will focus on the key areas that require understanding- budgeting, saving and credit. The goal is not to provide you with every single detail about financial literacy but to lay a foundation and plant interest in you developing a better understanding independently.

BUDGETING

If I offered you a check for one million dollars and asked you what you would do with it I am sure the responses would vary greatly. I love hearing when people say they would save or invest part and enjoy the other part. The concerning responses are when people say things that clearly indicate they do not understand budgeting. For example, I can take that one-million-dollar check and purchase a house that is $900,000 and would feel amazing. The question is- have you factored in other related expenses when purchasing the house- the property taxes, utilities, general maintenance, etc.? Without proper budgeting, that house will be gone before you have a chance to move any furniture into it.

Budgeting is one of the most fundamental practices that will ensure that you stay on top of your finances- from income to expenses. Without a budget, it is incredibly difficult to hold yourself accountable for where your money is coming from and where it is going. A budget can be set up whether you are only receiving an allowance, have a regular job or if you got money for your birthday or holiday. Asking yourself basic questions allows you to set up a budget- how much money do you have or are making consistently, what are your expenses and what are your savings goals?

As each of these factors can change, remember that a budget is not written in stone. It can and should be changed when circumstances change (ex.- you make or get more money or are able to save more). The goal is to try to stick to the budget you create as much as possible.

One of the biggest struggles in budgeting is differentiating between what you need and what you want. The priority needs to be to focus spending on what is needed before focusing on what you want. There are a ton of things that I am sure you want but the question is whether it is stuff you really need. Don't get me wrong- I am not saying you should not spend money on the things you want, especially if you deserve and have earned it. It is about being financially responsible and making smart decisions for today and tomorrow. I learned many years ago of the 50/30/20 rule for budgeting and put it into practice today. The rules is broken down like this: 50% of income is spent on needs, 30% is spent on wants and 20% is saved. For example, for every $100 you receive, you should be able to save $20, spent $30 on the things you want and spend $50 on what is needed. As budgets are meant to be flexible, if you have less needs one month then you can increase your savings or maybe make an extra want purchase.

Just remember that without a budget thing can easily go wrong and poor decisions can be made easily.

SAVING

A lack of financial literacy and money management makes saving money seem like an impossible task. A lack of discipline and a weak ability to resist temptation also contribute to the challenges of saving, for both adults and young people. In addition, emergencies in life that lead to unexpected expenses can also play a significant role in saving money. Saving money did not make sense to me until I understood it in a more practical way. The goal of saving is to stay ready for anything that comes our way- both good and bad. Whether it be an unplanned expense or an opportunity to purchase something unexpected- you can be ready with the right savings plan in place.

Complicating the process of saving can create hopelessness or confusion. I learned how to save in very basic steps and have grown these practices in different ways to increase my ability to save. To start, I would collect change anywhere I could find it and put it in a container that does not make it easy to remove money from (I always suggest a large water bottle we see on water coolers in stores and offices). The next stage for me was conditioning myself to save. I trained myself to look at $5 bills as if they were not money. Every time I got a $5 bill I would put it in the water jug along with the change. The final stage was that I would treat any money that I find or did not expect or plan on receiving as if it was not money and it would go directly in the water jug. Doesn't sound like much right? The first year I was able to do this I took the money I saved and went on vacation. Not bad right? Remember that even small steps are progress and steady growth will yield big returns as long as you are consistent.

For those readers who have bank accounts and use debit cards, there are apps on your smart phone that do the work for you and make the process of saving super easy. Apps such as Acorns or Stash allow you to save without having to actively do anything. Acorns rounds up your expenses and puts the extra change in an account for you. Stash allows you to schedule money to be taken out of your account on a monthly basis and saved for you (or you can invest it in stocks if you choose to). Both are effective ways to save and take the thought process out of it. These are just a couple of several apps that exist that help with savings- all you need to do is invest your time in learning about them and using them.

CREDIT & CREDIT CARDS

Credit and credit cards offer great risk but also great rewards if managed and understood properly. Your credit score, which is a number between 350 to 800 and indicates your likelihood to pay back a loan or debt, is one of the most criteria for most major financial decisions most adults make- renting an apartment, buying a house, purchasing a car or taking out a loan. The higher your score the most trustworthy you are considered. The goal is to understand and put into practice the process of building your credit score and thus your borrowing power. The risk is that it is very easy to fall into the trap of relying on credit cards too heavily which can result in very complicated debt.

One way to build credit is to properly manage credit cards. Credit cards allow you to purchase items by taking a virtual loan and then paying that loan back when you receive the monthly bill. If you pay the monthly bill on time and consistently then it increases your trustworthiness and thus your credit score increases. The issue with credit cards is that it is very easy to rely on them and abuse them, sometimes without even realizing it. It feels very different when you have to take money out of your pocket and give it away compared to when you swipe a card and you don't even feel like you spent anything. In addition, it is easy to use credit to purchase something that you normally would not be able to afford or do not have the money to purchase at that time. One of the most important rules I was taught about credit cards is that if I do not have enough money to purchase the item twice in cash then I should not purchase the item on credit once. This rule, among others, are very helpful to avoid ending up in a very tough situation that is difficult to get out of.

Another really important aspect of credit cards to be mindful of is the APR, or annual percentage rate, which is the price you pay to borrow money. When you borrow money there is usually interest that is added on the amount owed which is the additional price for borrowing. Some credit cards offer a 0% APR, which means there is no additional cost to borrow money using the card as long as you meet the terms, which is usually to pay on time. Most credit cards, sometimes as penalty for a late payment, can have APR rates as high as 24%. This means that the interest added at the end of the year is basically 24% of the balance that is owed on the credit card. For example, if you have a $1000 balance at a 24% APR then that means at the end f the year you would owe close to $240 in interest on top of your balance. Imagine the balance was bigger? Or if you had multiple credit cards? You can easily end up in a situation where you are paying way more than what you borrowed and for a very long time.

As stated previously, financial literacy is a critical topic and not one that can easily be broken down or explained in one chapter of a book. The goal is to lay a foundation and to increase your curiosity to learn more. Making money is only one part of the process- how you manage your money is just as important and needs to be mastered sooner rather than later.

CHAPTER 15

COMMUNITY SERVICE

"We make a living by what we get, but we make a life by what we give."

- *Winston Churchill*

Throughout early education, one important rule that teachers taught us was to always clean up after yourself. The reasoning behind this is to always make sure that we leave a place in just as good, if not better, shape than how we found it. While this premise started in the classroom, the reality is, this is an essential state of mind and approach in our communities as well. It is not about saying it is not my problem or let someone else figure it out. We must always invest energy in make the space around us better whether it benefits us or not. This is the core principle behind community service.

Community service not only benefits society but also prays an important role in your own life and personal development. Here are a few ways in which community service is truly beneficial-

CONNECT WITH THE COMMUNITY

The world is so much bigger than our homes, our blocks and our schools. There are so many people living around us, many of which need support in some way. By actively working within the community you are able to develop deeper connections with your community and the people in it.

CHANGES PERSPECTIVE ON LIFE

When we are facing issues and obstacles we are convinced that it is the worst of the worst. However, community service allows to help others who are in a less fortunate situation than we are. This has a tremendous impact on our perspective on our lives and life in general. Many of the things we complain about or take for granted would be blessings to many other people.

RAISE SOCIAL AWARENESS

By being actively engaged in community service we learn about the many issues that are facing our community. Many of these issues may not impact or affect us directly but if they exist within your community then they deserve your time and attention to address. An issue in your community that may not affect you today may affect you tomorrow or may be impacting people you care about. I know a lot of politicians who began their political careers by doing community service in their community and realizing how much change was needed and took on the challenge as adults.

PERSONAL AND PROFESSIONAL GROWTH

Community service not only feels amazing but it is so important that many schools have implemented community service hours as a requirement for graduation. Personally, you develop numerous skills and experience through community work that can lead to academic and professional opportunities. It is also an amazing way to meet people who you may not otherwise have met. Academically and professionally, community service looks amazing on a resume and significantly boosts your marketability for the position or opportunity.

There are so many amazing and truly impactful ways to engage in community services depending on what part of your community you are focusing on. Here are some examples:

- ❖ Volunteer in a soup kitchen or shelter (especially around the holidays)
- ❖ Volunteer at your local church
- ❖ Volunteer to help in your school (ex.-helping with events, setting up bulletin boards, etc.)
- ❖ Become a mentor or a tutor to someone younger
- ❖ Collect and donate needed items (clothing, non-perishable foods, school supplies, etc.)
- ❖ Volunteer at a nursery home and support the elderly

- ❖ Organize clothing, food or money drives to donate to charities
- ❖ Volunteer to coach or train a youth sports team
- ❖ Help to fix or plant gardens
- ❖ Help rake leaves or shovel snow (when needed)
- ❖ Volunteer for a not-for-profit or local library
- ❖ Volunteer in an animal shelter

Community service is an amazing way to not only give back and help others, but also to grow as a person, build valuable skills, and meet new people doing positive and inspiring work.

There are so many different ways to give back and you can easily find a way to do so that fits with your passion and interests.

QUOTES TO LIVE BY

I am a huge fan of insightful, inspirational, motivational, and empowering quotes. I can attempt to come up with clever and innovative ways of saying some really powerful things but sometimes you find those perfect words already stated.

Each person is influenced or moved by a particular quote or the meaning behind a quote. With this in mind I wanted to share some of my favorite quotes in the hopes that can play a positive role in your life. If few or none of these quotes impact you I strongly advise that you look for quotes of your own to motivate you.

*"It's NOT the job you DO, It's **how** you DO the job."*

-Anonymous

"Strive not to be a success, but rather to be of value."

-Albert Einstein

"Every strike brings me closer to the next home run."

-Babe Ruth

"A business that makes nothing but money is a poor business."

-Henry Ford

"Success is walking from failure to failure with no loss of enthusiasm."

-Winston Churchill

"It always seems impossible until it's done."

-Nelson Mandela

"Successful and unsuccessful people do not vary greatly in their abilities. They vary in their desires to reach their potential."

-John Maxwell

"It's not what you achieve, it's what you overcome. That's what defines your career."

-Carlton Fisk

"The bigger the dream, the harder the grind."

-Eric Thomas

"Work to become, not to acquire."

-Elbert Hubbard

"I've missed more than 9,000 shots in my career. I've lost almost 300 games. 26 times, I've been trusted to take the game winning shot and missed. I've failed over and over and over again in my life. And that is why I succeed."

-Michael Jordan

"You can't build a reputation on what you're going to do."

-Confucius

"Focus your time on building meaningful relationships. You can be the smartest person in the room, but if nobody wants to work with you, that doesn't matter."

-Mogo

"If you want to change attitudes, start with a change in behavior. In other words, begin to act the part, as well as you can, of the person you would rather be, the person you most want to become. Gradually, the old, fearful person will fade away."

-William Glasser

"Your attitude, not your aptitude, will determine your altitude."

-Zig Ziglar

"The longer I live, the more I realize the impact attitude has on life. Attitude to me is more important than facts. It is more important than the past, than education, than money, than circumstances, than failures, than successes, than what other people think or say or do. It is more important than appearance, giftedness or skill. It will make or break a company…a church…a home. The remarkable thing is we have a choice everyday regarding the attitude we will embrace for the day. We cannot change our past. We cannot change the fact that people will act in a certain way. We cannot change the inevitable. The only thing we can do is play on the one string we have, and that is our attitude. I am convinced that life is 10% what happens to me and 90% how I react to it. And so it is with you. We are in charge of our attitudes."

-Charles R. Swindoll

"Don't make a habit of choosing what feels good over what is good for you."

-Eric Thomas

"Your smile is your logo, your personality is your business card, how you leave others feeling after having an experience with you becomes your trademark."

-Anonymous

"Work like there is someone working twenty-four hours a day to take it all away from you."

-Mark Cuban

"When you want to succeed, as bad as you want to breathe, then you'll be successful."

-Eric Thomas

"You have an idea, a dream? Go for it, don't settle and don't let anyone tell you that you can't – opportunity is everywhere."

-Chrissy Sgourakis

"Be authentic, be you, and be the energy you want to attract."

-Julia Hame

"Don't be afraid to take chances early on. The more established you become within a particular field, the harder it'll be to break free."

-Ash Molaei

"Be okay with failing. The traditional route isn't for most of us. Learn from that failure and carve your own path."

-Christian Dare

"The only way to get out of mediocrity is to keep shooting for excellence."

-Eric Thomas

"It is literally true that you can succeed best and quickest by helping others to succeed."

-Napolean Hill

"The strongest thing that any human being has going for itself is its own integrity and it's own heart. As soon as you start veering away from that, the solidity that you need to stand up for what you believe in, just isn't going to be there."

-Herbie Hancock

"What lies behind us and what lies before us are small matters compared to what lies within us."

-Oliver Wendell Holmes

"Six essential qualities that are the key to success include sincerity, personal integrity, humility, courtesy, wisdom, and charity."

-Dr. William Menninger

"Whether you think you can, or you think you can't--you're right."

-Henry Ford

"The future rewards those who press on. I don't have time to feel sorry for myself. I don't have time to complain. I'm going to press on."

-Barack Obama

"Be Inspirational!"

-Richard Celestin, Esq.

ABOUT THE AUTHOR

Richard Anthony Celestin, Esq. was born and raised in Jamaica, Queens. He is living proof that adversity and obstacles can only strengthen and motivate us to achieve our dreams and goals.

As a small child, he experienced severe bullying due to his height and weight. In high school, he had to overcome a life-changing medical diagnosis that resulted in his hospitalization, numerous surgical attempts to repair complications, and several near-death experiences.

As a young professional, he lacked the focus and maturity to take advantage of the blessings that laid before him. Despite these odds, Richard remained focused on achieving his dreams with the ultimate goal of giving back to his community and sharing his life story and struggles as a source of inspiration.

Richard is a graduate of *The City University of New York (CUNY) School of Law*. While at CUNY Law, he focused his studies on criminal defense and juvenile justice. Prior to entering law school, and since becoming an attorney, he has directed his work towards underrepresented and at-risk youth via the not- for-profit sector and with alternative-to- detention programs in Manhattan, Brooklyn, and Queens. He offers his knowledge and insight into the juvenile and criminal justice areas by participating in panel discussions and conducting workshops throughout New York City addressing issues and concerns that affect communities of color, primarily the rising arrest and incarceration rates of youth of color.

In addition to working with youth involved in the juvenile and criminal justice systems, Richard created a limited liability corporation, **Richard Celestin Consulting Group, LLC,** for the purposes of developing and providing legal skill development, self-awareness, youth empowerment, and consequential thinking programs to elementary, middle and high school students in New York City, New Jersey and Long Island. Under the LLC, Richard operates the *Young Debaters Program*, which has been implemented in over 85 schools and focuses on teaching students the skills behind debate and oral advocacy. Richard also serves as a consultant for various organizations seeking to develop youth-based programs within the community, practices various

133

areas of the law, and is an adjunct professor at CUNY Queens College.

One of Richard's proudest moments to date is in the publication of his first book, *The Hard Facts About Soft Skills*. Knowing that his academic record was not sufficient to achieve the success he wanted and envisioned, Richard needed to develop and sharpen all the tools he had access to in order to remain competitive and relevant in the professional world. His second book, *Embracing Adversity: Finding Power and Strength in Life's Most Challenging Times,* is focused on his personal journey dealing with adversity and obstacles and provides practical advice on how to build resilience and stay motivated despite the challenges of life. As with any successful person, it is imperative that he shares his journey and the valuable skills he learned along the way. As a proud author, Richard plans on publishing more works focused on personal and professional growth.

To learn more information about my work and passion, to book a speaking engagement or workshop, or to stay in contact, please check out the following:

www.RichardCelestinLLC.com
RCelestinLLC@gmail.com
#youngdebatersprogram

www.TheInspirationalLawyer.com
TheInspirationalLawyer@gmail.com
IG: @the_inspirational_lawyer
#theinspirationallawyer

Made in the USA
Middletown, DE
05 November 2022

14185352R00077